Dolls

of

Three Centuries

BY

ELEANOR ST. GEORGE

*"The world is so full of a number of things,
I'm sure we should all be as happy as kings."*
—Robert Louis Stevenson

CHARLES SCRIBNER'S SONS, NEW YORK
CHARLES SCRIBNER'S SONS, LTD., LONDON
1951

TO FRANK

"There's rosemary, that's for remembrance"

Acknowledgments

One of the finest things about the doll collecting hobby is the generosity of collectors in sharing the bits of information that each has acquired in the course of his or her collecting. There is very much that we do not know and much that we probably may never know, but the generosity of other collectors has helped greatly.

Special thanks are due George C. Putnam of California, son of the late Grace Storey Putnam, for pictures and information about the life of his mother, for access to certain parts of her yet unpublished autobiography, and for the loan of a book on his father's life, *Arthur Putnam, Sculptor*.

To Monsieur Moynot, President of the Société Française de Fabrication des Bébés et Jouets (French Society for the Manufacturing of Dolls and Toys), go our thanks for information on the subsequent history of the Jumeau and Bru dolls, and also for his Christmas gift to our personal collection of two thirty-two-inch "Princess" dolls representing the Princesses Elizabeth and Margaret Rose of England. These dolls were designed in 1938 for King George and Queen Elizabeth to take back to their daughters as gifts from France when they visited President Loubet there just before the Second World War. The first pair of these "Princess" dolls that was imported to America is in the collection of Mrs. Gustav Mox of Santa Monica, California, and was exhibited at the National Doll Show at the Charles W. Bowers Memorial Museum at Santa Ana in 1949.

We are grateful to Mrs. Ruth Price of La Mesa, California, for putting us in touch with many California collectors and collections, and especially for introducing us to Mrs. Ruth Chase Howland, daughter of Mrs. Martha Jenks Chase, maker of the Chase dolls, who gave us interesting details of her mother's life and work.

We are indebted to Dr. Byron P. Merrick of Berlin Heights, Ohio, for pictures of the musical dolls in his fine collection of music boxes.

Miss Elizabeth MacMahon of Everett, Massachusetts, generously submitted pictures of her collection of antique Japanese festival dolls and allowed us access to her collection of rare books on Japanese dolls. Thanks are due also to Miss Anna V. Doyle of Jamaica Plains, Massachusetts, who purchased the outstanding collection of the late Miss Hendricks of Worcester, Massachusetts, and brought the entire collection of one hundred and fifty dolls down for us to see.

We are also grateful to Mrs. Imogene Anderson of New York City and to Mrs. Edna Fletcher of Newburgh, New York, for pictures of rare dolls from their collections. No dolls from either of these collections have been shown in any other doll book before.

To Mr. Harold Rugg, Assistant Librarian of the Baker Memorial Library at Hanover, New Hampshire, for an early catalogue of the Ludlow Doll Carriage factory from his collection of Vermontiana, we acknowledge our indebtedness. Also thanks are due the reference staff of the Baker Memorial Library of Dartmouth College for its research work.

We are indebted to "Mama" Clear, as usual, for advice, criticism and information, and especially for calling our attention to the remarkable doll work being done by Mrs. Gladys MacDowell in the Canal Zone.

Our thanks to Mr. and Mrs. Edmund Poetter for their help in many ways; to Mr. and Mrs. Grant J. Holt of Keene, New Hampshire, for exclusive pictures of the remarkable collection of dolls which they gathered from nine European countries; and to Mrs. Claire Ellegood Smith of Hancock, New Hampshire, for complete pictures of her unusual collection. To these and many other collectors, our thanks.

ELEANOR ST. GEORGE.

Sybilholme
Quechee, Vermont
June 10, 1951

Contents

Illustrations

Dolls of Three Centuries

Musical Dolls

WE call her "Suzette" and her charm is undeniable, appealing to old and young alike. A little waif in a nondescript costume, selling flowers on a Parisian street corner, her great brown eyes beseech you to buy and when the music box on which she stands begins to play "Who'll Buy My Flowers?", her left hand lifts the cover of her basket to display her wares. Then she slowly closes the lid of the basket, extends her right hand with a bunch of flowers, turns her head to the right and brings the bouquet to her face to smell the flowers, and then repeats the routine.

Suzette is a French Jumeau doll standing on a Swiss music box. Depending on where your interest lies, you would call Suzette a music box with a doll or a musical doll. If you collect music boxes, it will be the former. If you collect dolls, it will be the latter. Not all of these small boxes have dolls. Many have animals of different kinds.

Some of the boxes were made in Germany, some were made in France but for the most part the music boxes on which the dolls stand were made in Switzerland where the manufacture of musical mechanisms reached near perfection.

Some of the musical dolls came to America, of course, but the majority are still to be found in Europe. Mr. and Mrs. Grant J. Holt of Keene, New Hampshire, while doll collecting in Paris, found an antique shop whose owner told them that at one time during World War II he had had sixty of these musical dolls, brought in from the country dis-

1

tricts by G. I.'s. In America, they are comparatively rare and really good collections may have only one or two, or even none at all.

The Jumeau dolls were frequently used on music boxes. Dr. Byron P. Merrick of Berlin Heights, Ohio, who is a collector of music boxes, has one with a Jumeau doll dressed as Little Red Ridinghood. She holds over her arm the basket of food that she is taking to her grandmother.

Miss Anna V. Doyle of Jamaica Plains, Massachusetts, has a Jumeau doll dressed as a fine lady. She has a bouquet in her left hand and a black lace fan in the other. When the music box plays she alternately fans herself and raises the bouquet to her nose. This music box plays two tunes.

In the same picture with this doll are two German music boxes, the one with a clown performing on a ladder, the other with a parade of children. This is pulled along by a string so that the children seem to be marching while the music plays. This box is not automatic.

The Jumeau doll was always distinguishable by its unusually fine large eyes and by this standard cannot be mistaken for anything else. There are at least five musical dolls in the dozen or more that Mr. and Mrs. Grant J. Holt brought from Paris in December, 1949, that are Jumeaus. These can be thus described:

1. Musical Jumeau doll in Normandy costume with wooden shoes. As the music plays, the doll does a sort of tap dance and her hands move vertically while her head moves from side to side.

2. Musical Jumeau doll. A little girl with a bird cage. When the music plays the bird moves up and down in its cage as if singing. The doll's head moves from side to side and the hand which is not holding the cage moves up and down. The ornaments on the doll's dress are cherries and her eyes are brown. A label underneath the music box has the name "Jumeau."

3. A musical Jumeau doll with flowers. She is nineteen inches tall and has blue eyes.

4. Musical Jumeau boy doll with blue-gray eyes. As the music plays, the hand holding a cigarette comes up as if he were smoking and his head tilts back.

5. Musical Jumeau doll with egg. She is eighteen inches tall. As the music plays, she moves the egg from left to right, while her other hand moves up and down. At the same time her head moves from side to side. Her eyes are brown and her hair is blonde.

Left, "Suzette," a musical Jumeau doll of about 1870, representing a waif selling
   flowers on the streets of Paris
St. George Collection

Right, Jumeau musical doll: Flower girl similar to Suzette
Collection of Mrs. Charles Doherty, Worcester, Mass.

Another very intriguing musical doll in the Holt collection is a little
girl standing behind an octagonal table. She has a doll in her right hand
and a string in her left hand; a kitten is on the music box at her feet. As
the music box plays "Ma Petite Bourgeoise," she brings the doll slowly
to her face as if kissing it, then dangles the ball of string in her left hand
in front of the kitten which plays with the string.

A Jumeau doll quite similar to Suzette, but which apparently has been
re-dressed by some former owner, is in the collection of Mrs. Charles
Doherty of Worcester, Massachusetts. It was formerly in the collection
of the late Mrs. Grace Garland, the well-known doll collector and dealer
in Worcester. After the deaths of Mrs. Garland's husband and sister,
during Mrs. Garland's long illness when she was alone in the world, her
neighbor, Mrs. Charles Doherty, cared for her as a devoted sister might

3

have. When Mrs. Garland passed on it was discovered that she had willed her beautiful dolls to her neighbor.

In the course of collecting, this author had bought many dolls from Mrs. Garland. Among them was the beautiful bisque Jumeau doll "Little Eva," named for the heroine of the then best-seller, Harriet Beecher Stowe's *Uncle Tom's Cabin*. The doll was brought from Paris in 1869 by Captain Webb on the maiden voyage of his clipper ship "Rosie Webb." He brought it as a gift for his daughter, Rosie, for whom the ship had been named, and who later became Mrs. Rose Webb Davis of Rockland, Maine. She kept the doll until her fiftieth wedding anniversary and then sold it to Mrs. Grace Garland. The story is told in *The Dolls of Yesterday*, except for one fact. Mrs. Garland sold the doll to us on the condition that we did not tell anybody where we had got it, as she feared it might hurt Mrs. Davis to know that the doll was in other hands.

Shortly before Mrs. Garland's death we advertised in *Yankee Magazine's* Swoppers' Column for an old-fashioned pinking iron, and among the replies we received was one from Mrs. Rose Webb Davis of Rockland, Maine. We had a wonderful correspondence with Mrs. Davis and when Mrs. Garland died we felt released from our promise of silence, rightly thinking that Mrs. Davis would be happy to know that "Little Eva" was in safe and loving hands. She was.

A lovely Jumeau, shown through the courtesy of Mrs. Mariemae Schwartz, pours tea into cups on the tray she holds before her while the music box on which she stands plays. A more recent musical bisque in the collection of Mariemae Schwartz is dated by her open lips and teeth. (Bisques prior to the early 1880's had closed lips and no teeth.) She is further dated by the fact that one of the two tunes played by her music box is the "Merry Widow Waltz." Possibly this richly be-jewelled doll is intended to represent the "Merry Widow" herself.

A very unusual musical doll, of which we have a photograph through the courtesy of B. H. Leffingwell, a dealer in Rochester, New York, is a Chinese mandarin, or, it may be a Chinese lady. The left hand, with whatever it may have held, is missing and so is the wig. The music played is a sort of Chinese tune.

Another unusual item, perhaps more music box than doll, is a Holy Family in the collection of Dr. Byron P. Merrick of Berlin Heights, Ohio. It plays Christmas airs.

Jumeau musical doll, Little Red Ridinghood
Collection of Dr. Byron P. Merrick, Berlin Heights, Ohio

Left, Jumeau musical doll: Little girl in Normandy dress

Right, Jumeau musical doll: Little girl with a bird cage
Both from the collection of Mrs. Grant J. Holt, Keene, New Hampshire

Many of the music boxes have one or more dancing dolls on them. One of these is in the collection of Mrs. Catherine Richards Howard of Hope, Arkansas. Another in the collection of Dr. Merrick has four dancing dolls.

On an earlier trip to Europe, the Holts brought back several musical dolls, one of which is a little girl who manipulates a puppet show while the music plays. Another is a little boy who powders his nose and admires himself in the mirror he holds.

Of course in a sense, all these musical dolls are really music boxes. But they fit equally well into both types of collections since the mechanism which controls the music also controls certain motions of the dolls.

While the music boxes are generally Swiss, as mentioned before, it is quite obvious that the combination of music boxes and dolls is of French origin. When it has not been destroyed, there is generally a label pasted on the bottom of the box naming the tune that the music box plays. These labels are in French and the tunes are almost always

6

Left, Jumeau musical doll: Little boy smoking

Right, Jumeau musical doll: Little girl with flowers
Both from the collection of Mrs. Grant J. Holt, Keene, New Hampshire

French tunes—often old ones—which seems to confirm the idea that the majority of musical dolls were created in Paris. Most of them seem to date to about 1870.

A later type of musical doll dates from about 1908. This type is mounted on a handle. Twirling the doll about with a circular motion causes the music to play. One pair of these in the collections of the author and of Mrs. Edmund Poetter is illustrated in the drawing included in this chapter. The parts are German but apparently were assembled in France. The little bisque heads are very lovely. One has a Kammer and Reiner head, the other head is marked "A and M" which stands for Armand Marseilles. Both firms have made wonderful bisque heads. The eyes of the one are blue, and of the other, gray.

A more recent musical doll is Bernard Ravca's organ grinder which was first displayed at Lord & Taylor's store in New York City in 1938. In the organ is a mechanism which when wound up plays the French national anthem, "La Marseillaise."

7

The companion of this doll is a pedlar woman, the wife of the organ grinder. Her picture is shown in the chapter on pedlar dolls. Mr. Ravca has also done a fascinating group of figures representing the players of various instruments in an orchestra, but they can hardly be called "musical dolls" in the strict sense, because the dolls are all silent.

Left, Jumeau musical doll: Little girl with egg

Right, French musical doll: Little girl with doll and kitten
Both from the collection of Mrs. Grant J. Holt, Keene, New Hampshire

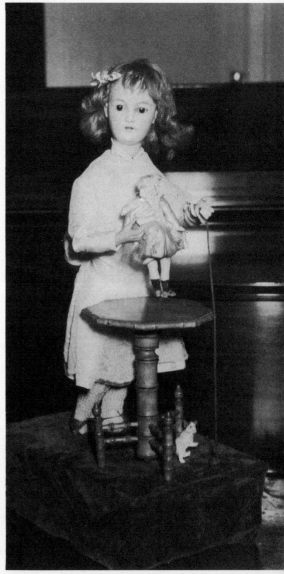

Musical Jumeau doll
Courtesy of Mrs. Mariemae Schwartz,
Cincinnati, Ohio

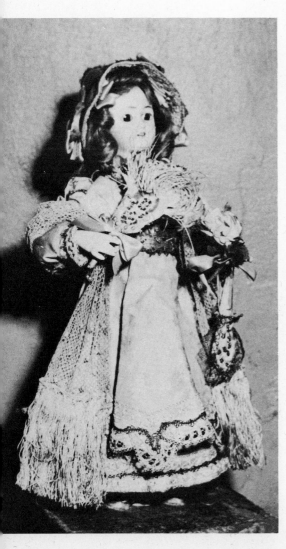

A more recent musical doll
Collection of Mrs. Mariemae Schwartz,
Cincinnati, Ohio

Left to right—
1. Musical Jumeau doll
2. German musical dolls: "The Parade"
3. German musical doll: Clown on a ladder
Collection of Miss Anna V. Doyle, Jamaica Plains, Mass.

Holy Family. Music box plays Christmas airs.
Collection of Dr. Byron P. Merrick, Berlin Heights, Ohio

Musical doll: Chinese mandarin or Chinese lady
Courtesy of B. H. Leffingwell, Rochester, New York

French musical doll. Little boy with mirror and powder puff.
Collection of Mr. and Mrs. Grant J. Holt, Keene, New Hampshire

Little girl with puppet show
Collection of Mr. and Mrs. Grant J. Holt, Keene, New Hampshire

Musical organ grinder which plays "La Marseillaise"
Courtesy of Bernard M. Ravca

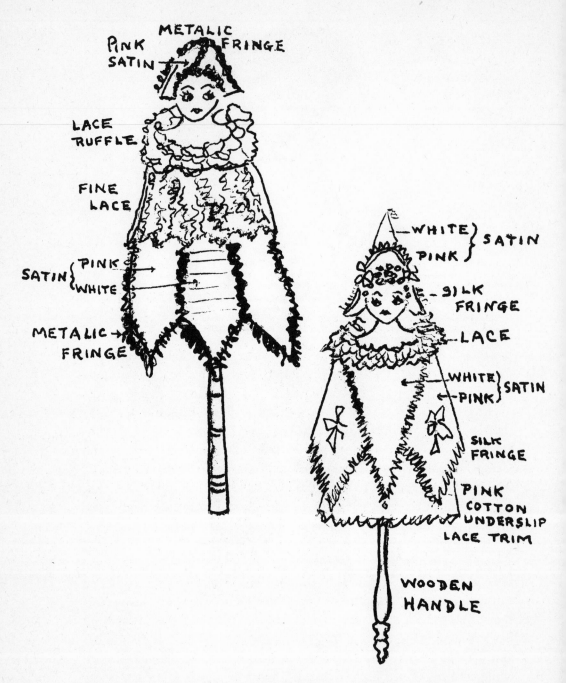

German bisque musical dolls, made about 1908. Music plays when doll is twirled by hand
Collections of Mrs. Edmund Poetter, Reading, Vermont, and Mrs. Eleanor St. George, Quechee, Vermont

2

Mechanical Dolls

THE Germans have always been especially skillful in the making of mechanical toys. One such clever toy has mice running around a kitchen, being chased by the cook with a carving knife. At the Crystal Palace exposition in London in 1851, one of the mechanical exhibits from Germany was a branch of a tree on which birds rested and then, when wound up, the birds flew from branch to branch.

France also made fascinating mechanical toys, and still does, from the reports of Mr. William Neuberger, promotional manager for the entire French toy industry. There is one establishment in Paris, Des Camps, which has been creating mechanical toys for three generations. Among their ingenious contrivances is a monkey that actually smokes. This is quite likely the source of the smoking courtier, an old French mechanical doll which Mrs. Emma Clear told us of restoring.

In the collection of Mrs. Grant J. Holt of Keene, New Hampshire, are two mechanical dolls brought from Paris. One of these is a lady doll ten and one-half inches tall. She stands on what looks like a three-wheeled cart without sides. At the back of the cart is the mechanism which causes the wheels to turn and makes the doll appear to be walking. Meanwhile, her left hand comes up and brings her lorgnette to her eyes, then drops and her right hand moves up and down as if she were fanning herself while her head moves forward and also turns. Her head is French bisque and she has beautiful blue eyes and white hair.

The second doll also has a bisque head and the mechanism in her body winds with a key. Then you press a lever on the other side of the body which releases the mechanism. This starts two chains going around on opposite sides of the body. These are connected to two rolls under the doll's feet which revolve to make the doll walk. At some time when she is walking, the bellows above the mechanism makes a crying sound. The head moves from side to side and the arms swing, as yours do when you walk.

Somewhat similar is a modern German walking doll from the collection of Marian L. Smith of Burlington, Vermont. This doll is twenty-two and one-half inches tall and is marked:

GERMANY
D.E.P.
101
2.

She is shown both undressed and dressed.

A walking doll of the 'sixties, with which most collectors are familiar, is the "Autoperipatetikos" walking doll. The one illustrated here is from the collection of the Warren County Historical Society, Lebanon, Ohio. The doll was bought for his little daughter by Captain Parshall, a hero of Warren County, just before he was killed in the Battle of Chickamauga.

Another walking doll that dates from the 1860's is one which pushes a small cart before her. The head and hands are papier-mâché, the doll is metal. There is no wind-up mechanism, but one starts it on the level with a little push and prongs on the feet which catch into the carpet propel the doll forward, pushing the cart ahead of her.

Another type of mechanical doll is one that talks. In 1887 or 1888, Thomas A. Edison, the inventor of the phonograph, adapted a phonograph with round disks for a doll. The result was a talking doll whose conversation could be changed by merely changing the disk. The pictures of this bisque doll are shown here by the courtesy of the Thomas Alva Edison Foundation of West Orange, New Jersey.

George Borgfeldt and Company, large importers and also manufacturers of dolls, being queried about the phonograph doll, stated that in 1907 or 1908 they had a sample celluloid doll with a phonograph and took some orders for it but the jobber was never able to make delivery on it.

French walking doll, found in Paris
Collection of Mr. and Mrs. Grant J. Holt, Keene, New Hampshire

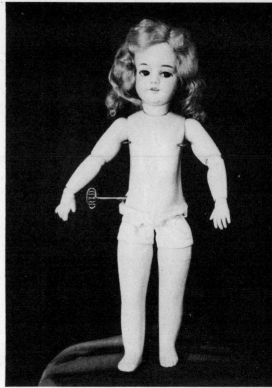

1   2

M. J. S. Moynot, President of the Société Française de Fabrication des Bébés et Jouets of Paris, states that they made a phonograph doll as a novelty for the Paris Exposition of 1900. The company abandoned the making of this doll after the Exposition as it cost too much to be profitable. The only one of these dolls made by the Edison Company of which we know is in private hands so it is safe to assume that not many of them were made in America either.

An interesting old French mechanical toy, in original condition and still in its original box, is "Le Gai Violiniste" in the collection of Mr. and Mrs. Erwin Chapin of Silver Creek, New York. The doll winds with a key and when it is wound up the man moves his arm back and forth, drawing the bow across the strings of the violin.

A walking doll of American design and manufacture, "Dolly Walker," has been written up in only one doll book, in one of the manuals of the Doll Collectors of America, where it is credited to Mrs. Emma C. Clear of the Humpty Dumpty Doll Hospital, Redondo Beach, California. Although the patent, now lapsed, stood in Mrs. Clear's name, she did not, as a matter of fact, invent the doll. It was invented by Harry Cole-

3

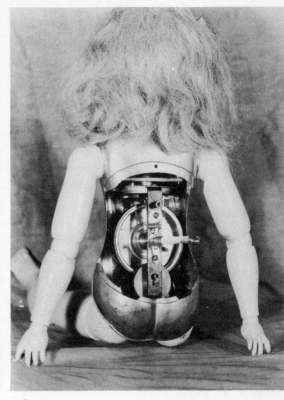

4

1. German walking doll made after 1898 and marked "Germany"
Collection of Marian L. Smith, Burlington, Vermont

2. German walking doll without her clothes
Collection of Marian L. Smith, Burlington, Vermont

3. Edison phonograph doll, 1887-1888
Courtesy of Thomas Alva Edison Foundation, West Orange, New Jersey

4. Detail of the Edison phonograph doll
Courtesy of Thomas Alva Edison Foundation, West Orange, New Jersey

5. French mechanical doll which walks and moves her arms
Collection of Mr. and Mrs. Grant J. Holt, Keene, New Hampshire

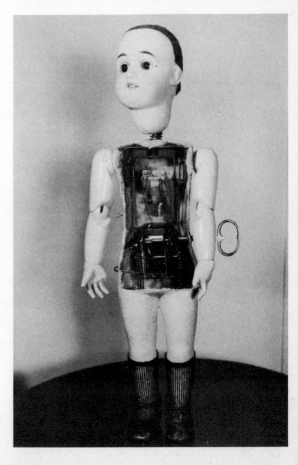

5

man, a ventriloquist on the vaudeville stage, whose dummy walked with him. The dummy was about the size of a fourteen-year-old boy. Both strolled onto the stage in evening clothes, sat down and went through the usual patter. The act went over so well that he decided to make the dummies with the walking mechanism in doll size.

This is the story as Mrs. Clear tells it: "For a year or so, we furnished him (Harry Coleman) some of the parts. He wanted us to carry it, but I like beautiful dolls and disliked that one, so we turned it down. Then we moved from Hill Street to Broadway and Harry said we simply had to carry it. Again I turned him down. He had consigned a lot of them to the department stores but they simply could not sell them. The doll had to be demonstrated.

"Our location was ideal. We had the second floor on the east side of Broadway. The first floor was located so that the crowds on the west side of the street looked directly into our windows. Harry was playing at the Pantageous Theatre across the street. He planned to take out one of the big plate glass windows and use the ledge for demonstrating the doll. He would come over between the acts at the theatre and put on a combination doll show and ventriloquist act. We fell for it and from then on life became one grand circus.

"Several baby movie stars came up to take part in the show. He would walk them out on that ledge and they would walk stiff-legged like the dolls. My son was in high school and we had a bunch of high school boys putting in part time work. I had a brain storm. I promised to pay for their dinners if each boy would walk a doll down Broadway to the cafeteria. My son said he would starve to death before he would walk down Broadway leading a doll. Some of the others wanted to know the limits on the eats. I told them no limit just so they did not waste any food. They had probably been spending twenty-five cents each. It cost me seventy-five to eighty cents each. Christie, my son, finally fell for the fun of it as did the others. We made every downtown cop a present of a doll. We did not want any argument about impeding traffic.

"We had passes to the theatre and Harry asked us to come in during his act but we were always too busy. One night as we left the cafeteria, we noticed that it was just about time for his act, so we went in. There was the regular act with the big dummy. Then he walked into the wings with it, and came back carrying a doll in each hand, one in pink, the

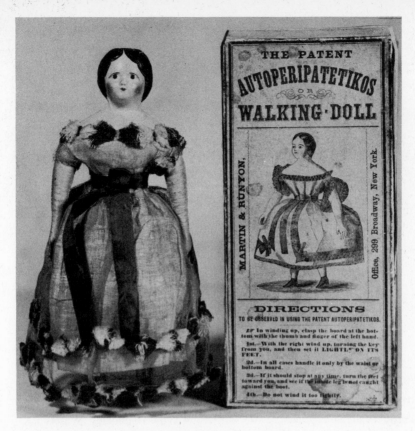

"Autoperipatetikos" walking doll
Collection of Warren County Historical Society, Lebanon, Ohio

other in blue. He danced them. Then he put on a baby ventriloquist act. Then he asked the audience if they liked them. The house roared its approval. 'Well, if you want one you can get it right across the street at the doll hospital. By the way, we have the doll lady and her husband with us tonight,' and he introduced us. After that we could not very well leave at once.

"When we got back, the store was crowded and while Harry demonstrated the dolls, everybody else was busy wrapping them up. I saw their possibilities if properly handled.

"Harry was leaving for the East. His wife had a new baby and wanted to be out of dolls. So I bought the patent rights, paying him a thousand dollars for them and some six or seven hundred dollars for the stock of parts. The new arrangement would be the reverse of the old one; we would make and furnish the dolls and Harry would sell them and demonstrate them on commission. He was to be booked in Los Angeles some six weeks before the following Christmas. Pantageous was a friend of his, which is why he allowed him to talk from the stage.

23

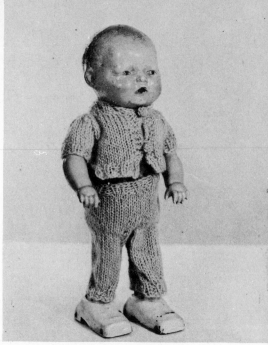

Left, Old French mechanical toy, "Le Gai Violiniste"
Collection of Mrs. Erwin Chapin, Silver Creek, New York

Right, Walking doll made by the Waterbury Watch Company, Waterbury,
    Connecticut
Courtesy of W. B. Mollard, Westfield, New York

"Then we lost our town location when some eastern syndicate bought
the building. They wanted six hundred dollars a month for the same
space in the new building that we had paid only one hundred twenty
five for in the old—much too high for a seasonal business. We took the
business to our home. Letters that we wrote to Harry came back un-
opened. I wrote to Alexander Pantageous and he replied that Harry was
dead—had died suddenly in December shortly after he left California.
So, with no downtown location and no demonstrator, that doll was out
and I put it out of my mind as another dead horse for which I had paid
a thousand dollars.

"When Janet Johl wrote me about dolls made during the World
War I period, I completely forgot about this one. The Doll Collectors of
America, when preparing the material for their 1940 supplement to
American Made Dolls and Figurines, dug the patent out of the Patent
Office.

"The body of the original doll was a crude affair of screen wire and
lath and had jointed knees. Mr. Clear, at the solicitation of a customer,
24

Walking doll
Courtesy of B. H. Leffingwell, Rochester, New York

made a new and different body, a slender cloth body without joints at
the knees. This was much better and we were all set to go with it when
World War II came and put a stop to everything."

This then, is the story of "Dolly Walker."

The Waterbury Watch Company of Waterbury, Connecticut, made
a very few mechanical toys including a walking doll, which we are privileged to show here by courtesy of W. B. Mollard, antique dealer in
Westfield, New York. It is still in perfect mechanical condition. The
doll is a little boy about four years old, all metal. The stocky little fellow
is about twelve inches tall, with a head about like a medium-sized apple.
He has decidedly oversized feet in which is concealed a pair of rollers
near the heels, similar to those of roller skates. He steps out forthrightly
and sturdily as he walks, after being wound with a key at his waist. The
doll is undoubtedly rare. Probably few were made, and fewer still have
survived. The successors of the Waterbury Watch Company, when
queried about this doll, said they had no means of finding out anything
about it. Certainly it is one of a very few American-made walking dolls.

25

The Subsequent History of the Jumeau and Bru Dolls

DURING recent years, a number of doll collectors and doll hospitals have been puzzled by the appearance from time to time of some dolls whose heads would be marked "Bru," and whose bodies would be marked "Jumeau," or vice versa. Even so knowledgeable a person as Mrs. Emma Clear was of the opinion that it indicated a close relationship between the houses of Jumeau and Bru, if they were not, indeed, one and the same house. In this, "Mama" Clear, as doll collectors all over the country call her, was partly right and partly wrong.

Determined to get to the bottom of the mystery, we contacted the French Embassy in Washington. They in turn referred us to their Information Bureau in New York which gave us two addresses. One was that of the French equivalent of the United States Patent Office and the other was the address of the Société Française de Fabrication des Bébés et Jouets, 160 rue Picpous, Paris. The French patent office wrote that all French patents were recorded in the United States Patent Office in Washington. This fact apparently was not known by the various researching doll collectors who for years past have combed the patents for dolls.

M. J. S. Moynot, president of the Société Française de Fabrication des Bébés et Jouets (French Society for the Manufacture of Dolls and Toys), was most courteous, replying to several letters and setting us straight on many questions. He gave a clear explanation of the toymaking situation in France.

Up to the year 1898, the houses of Jumeau and Bru were separate—business rivals, in fact. In 1898, they ceased to exist as entities and, with other toymaking enterprises, were merged to form a large corporation called La Société Française de Fabrication des Bébés et Jouets. Two daughters of M. Jumeau and a son-in-law of M. Bru were elected among the directors of the new corporation and still hold their offices.

In 1938, the Bru doll ceased to be manufactured but the Jumeau doll is still being made, with various changes and improvements. Needless to say, these changes and improvements have been such that the present day Jumeau bears little or no resemblance to the old, collector's Jumeau which was made by the old firm. No one could possibly mistake one for the other. Of course the new Jumeau dolls are also "collectors' items" even though they bear little resemblance to the old. Each has its distinguishing features.

The foregoing is in the nature of what newspaper men call a "scoop" —for so far as we know, no one before has stated these facts regarding the Bru and Jumeau dolls for the information of American collectors.

Although M. Moynot did not specifically say so, there is little doubt that in the merger each house turned over a considerable number of unused parts, heads, bodies, etc., and that these were not discarded but put together in various combinations.

Not all these hybrids conformed to the Bru-Jumeau combinations, undoubtedly because other firms merged with the Société at the same time. Mrs. R. C. Helsing of Oak Park, Illinois, has a beautiful bisque-headed doll with a kid body which is quite unusual. On the head is the deeply incised mark:

S & H COMPANY
Germany
D. E. P.

Beneath this is a red oval stamp with an incised letter. On the left shoulder is incised the usual Bru mark:

B
R
U
JUNIOR

These markings indicate several things: S & H is the mark of Simon and Halbig—well known German doll makers. "Germany" indicates that the head was made after 1898, when the United States Congress passed the law requiring all imported goods to be stamped with the name of the country of origin.

The name "Bru Junior" being incised on the left shoulder—the usual place for such a mark—must have been incised in Germany. A tenable theory is that a Bru head, broken above the swivel neck, was replaced by an S & H head by some later owner. We have seen a similar Bru doll from which the head was broken off above the swivel neck. The shoulder has the incised Bru mark and the body is one of the finest kid bodies we have ever seen. This broken doll is in the collection of Mr. and Mrs. Ben Holt of New Britain, Connecticut. The Holts are searching diligently for a Bru head.

In 1938, when the King and Queen of England visited President Loubet of France just prior to World War II, the Société Française de Fabrication de Bébés et Jouets made special Jumeau dolls for them to take home to the little English princesses. The dolls represented Princess Elizabeth and Princess Margaret Rose. The dolls were especially made at the order of the French government. They had elaborate wardrobes packed in fifteen blue leather doll trunks which were silver mounted. According to M. Moynot, some twenty pairs of the Princess dolls have since come to the United States.

The first pair of these lovely Princess dolls to be brought to America was imported by Bullock's Department Store of Los Angeles and sold into the outstanding collection of Mrs. Gustav Mox of Santa Monica, California. She exhibited them at the National Doll Show of 1949 at the Charles W. Bowers Memorial Museum at Santa Ana, California, where they were much admired.

The second set, so far as we know, was the one sent to the author's collection as a gift from M. Moynot. These dolls are thirty-two inches tall. Princess Elizabeth has dark hair and a lovely sheer white dress embroidered with bouquets of pastel colored flowers. The Princess Margaret Rose has blonde hair and her dress is pale blue. Both dolls have wigs of real hair. The eyes are marvelous—moving from side to side ("flirting eyes") as well as up and down (sleeping eyes). They have real eyelashes. M. Moynot also included in his gift to us, a twelve-inch modern Jumeau doll.

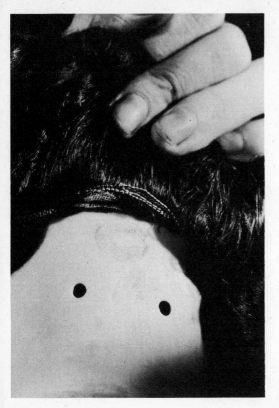

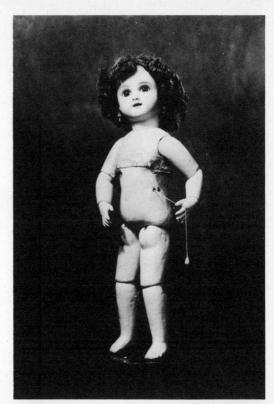

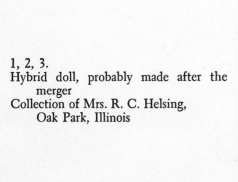

1, 2, 3.
Hybrid doll, probably made after the
    merger
Collection of Mrs. R. C. Helsing,
    Oak Park, Illinois

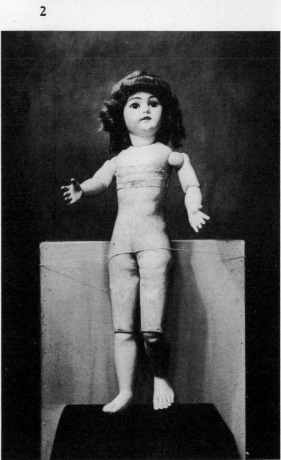

1

2

3

The Princess Dolls: Lovely thirty-two inch French bisques of the Princesses
Margaret Rose (*left*) and Elizabeth (*right*)
St. George Collection

Jumeau doll with today's modern improvements
Courtesy of Société Française de Fabrication des Bébés et Jouets

Mr. and Mrs. Grant Holt of Keene, New Hampshire, who brought many dolls from Europe, came home with the Princess dolls in a smaller size for their collection. No doubt when other collectors see these modern Jumeau dolls there will be many collections that will include them—for they are very lovely.

French dolls by a variety of makers
Collection of Mrs. F. F. Hockaday, Medford, Massachusetts

M. Moynot has all the molds of the original Jumeau dolls, and each year plans to issue for collectors replicas of these dolls in limited quantities. Each doll will be numbered and dated and each will have the wardrobe of a French fashion doll. These, in time, will probably be considered as valuable as the old French fashion dolls. The original molds of the Bru dolls are not available.

Contemporaries of Bru and Jumeau were a number of minor French doll makers. In the group picture of the interesting collection of Mrs. F. F. Hockaday of Medford, Massachusetts, are, besides old Jumeaus, old French dolls marked: S. B. J. F., R. D., W. D. & E. D., Fr. Greffier, Steiner, Limoges, "J. V." in an anchor. A number are simply marked "Déposée," which means the same thing as our "Patent Applied For." "Déposée" may often indicate that the doll is a Jumeau.

The old Jumeau was the acme of French doll-making art and there is no mistaking it for any other French doll. In the group is also included the "Bébé Steiner" which many collectors have considered a French

32

doll. We understand on the authority of M. Moynot, however, that it is not a French doll, but merely assembled in France from parts made in Germany.

We have an illustration of how unmistakable is the Jumeau type in the doll pictured here belonging to Mrs. Philip Cummings of Woodstock, Vermont. Mrs. Cummings discovered it in the attic in a box of dolls that had been her mother's. Her daughters, Lee, aged eleven, and Sarah, eight, who had visited the author's collection, immediately chorused: "Why she has just the same kind of eyes as Mrs. St. George's musical doll. She must be the same kind of doll." She was a Jumeau, identification proved. She is marked simply "Déposée."

This doll is also an example of something else. Prior to 1880, practically all Jumeau dolls were grown-up types. But when the rubber strung composition body was made (said to have been invented about 1880 by M. Jumeau's son), there were many little girl types such as this one among the Jumeaus, and their clothes were little girl clothes. These dolls almost invariably had earrings, as this one has, which helps to fix the date of the little girl dolls. In the early 1880's it was quite the mode to pierce the ears of small girls and fit them with earrings, the piercing of the ear lobes being considered beneficial to the child's eyes.

It is not known whether Jumeau or Bru invented the all wood jointed body which preceded the composition body. Both used it and either may have invented it. An example of this type of body is the set of charming eleven-inch Bru twins that belong to Miss Marion Howard and Miss Nellie D. MacLachlan, formerly partners in The Doll House, Miami, Florida.

Some collectors and some dealers speak of "French Fashion Dolls" as though they were a class by themselves. Of course, they are nothing of the sort. They are merely good French dolls, like Jumeaus and Brus, which have elaborate clothes typifying the mode of the moment.

When we speak of French dolls we are most apt to be thinking of the lovely French bisques, but it must not be forgotten that the French made other types. One is the doll made of thick waxes which is discussed in Chapter 6 and which is quite as fine as the Montanari wax doll. More rare than either the bisque or the wax doll is a very fine composition doll with painted hair. It is smoother and finer than any German composition doll. Mr. and Mrs. Grant J. Holt found in Paris six of these composition

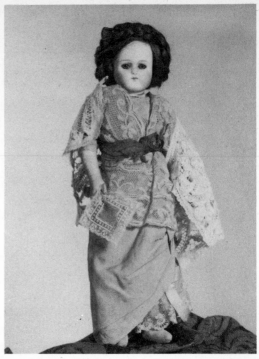

Left, Jumeau doll brought from Paris in 1884
Collection of Mrs. Philip Cummings, Woodstock, Vermont

Right, Old Jumeau doll
Collection of Mrs. Ruth Price, La Mesa, California

dolls, some with painted hair and some with real hair wigs over the painted hair. These are as beautifully dressed as any French fashion doll. Some American collectors believed these dolls to be German, but the workmanship is so fine that there is no doubt they are of French manufacture. They are quite rare. Dolls covered with enamel, which have considerable charm, are also among the treasures which the Holts brought back from Paris.

A lovely bisque that was shown at the National Doll Show of 1949 is from the collection of Mrs. E. S. Carmick of Long Beach, California. Hers is a collection rich in beautiful bisque dolls. The outstanding feature of this particular doll is her real hair wig which falls in long curls.

Somewhat similar in construction to these are French portrait dolls belonging to Mrs. Lydia Bowerman of Milan, Ohio. The unique picture of Marie Antoinette is shown here. A second is a portrait doll of Queen Victoria which on the inside is dated 1850. The third is also a portrait doll but the identity of the subject is unknown. They all appear to have been made about the same date.

34

Left, French fashion doll

Right, French fashion doll (*back view*)
Collection of Miss Anna V. Doyle, Jamaica Plains, Massachusetts

Another interesting fashion doll is in the collection of Miss Anna V. Doyle of Jamaica Plains, Massachusetts and is unusual because it is dressed in the little plaid dress of a school girl. Although the author also has a Jumeau in an original pink taffeta, teen-age dress with pinked ruffles, such French fashion dolls are rare. Miss Doyle's doll was in the Hendricks Collection in Worcester, Massachusetts, which Miss Doyle purchased after the death of the owner.

Jumeau dolls are always lovely, even when they no longer wear their original French costumes. An old Jumeau which belonged to her aunt is a treasured possession of Mrs. Ruth Price of La Mesa, California. It is pictured here as re-dressed by Mrs. Price herself. The doll has a wig of auburn, human hair.

The eyes of Jumeau dolls are lovely, especially the brown ones. An old Jumeau doll was recently re-dressed for the author by Mrs. Ralph E. Wakeman of Claremont, New Hampshire. The design of the dress was copied from *Two Centuries of French Fashion** from the exquisite

* *Two Centuries of French Fashion* by Michelle Murphy. Charles Scribner's Sons, New York, 1950.

French dolls that were sent to America as a "Thank You" gift to America for their help in World War II. The material of which Mrs. Wakeman made the dress is pale lavender faille trimmed with narrow purple velvet ribbon. The flop hat of purple velvet was copied from the picture also. Mrs. Wakeman added black and white cameo earrings and pin, creating as lovely a costume as any French doll maker could.

Marie Antoinette
Collection of Mrs. Lydia Bowerman, Milan, Ohio

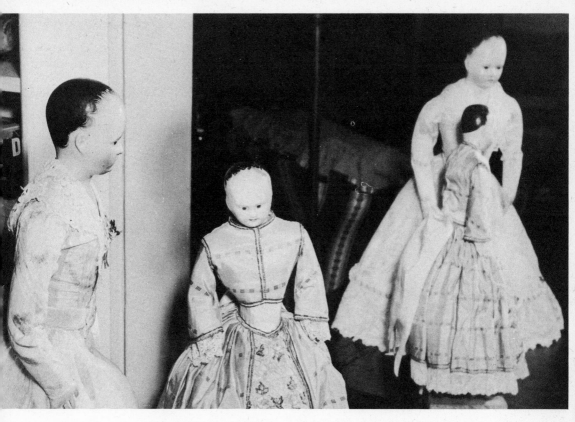

Above, Rare French composition dolls with painted heads and pink kid bodies

Below, the Holt French composition dolls with full headdress
All from the collection of Mr. and Mrs. Grant J. Holt, Keene, New Hampshire

Large bisque doll as displayed at
the National Doll Show,
1949
Collection of Mrs. E. S. Carmick, Long Beach, California

Jumeau doll costumed by Mrs.
Ralph E. Wakeman after
plate from *Two Centuries
of French Fashion* by Mi-
chelle Murphy
St. George Collection

4

Grace Storey Putnam

WHEN Grace Storey Putnam, creator of the Bye-lo Baby, died February 22, 1948 from a stroke suffered February 7, the art world lost not only a great doll designer but a competent artist and an illustrator of great versatility. Although Mrs. Putnam had a very full life, she will be chiefly remembered by that miracle of helpless infancy, the Bye-lo Baby, the original of which is now owned by her daughter.

The story of how she modelled it from a new-born infant in a Salvation Army Home is told by Mrs. Putnam herself in Janet Johl's first book, *The Fascinating Story of Dolls*. Two days before she was stricken, Mrs. Putnam completed her autobiography, which is now being edited for publication by her son, George Putnam.

Grace Storey was born in San Diego, California, March 16, 1877, the eldest of six children. When their mother died at the age of thirty-five, the children went to live with their grandparents, Mr. and Mrs. Daniel Choate, in their fine old mansion in San Diego. She was educated in the San Diego schools, with possibly two years of high school. But from the time she was eight years old, Grace Storey wanted to be an artist. Her grandfather, a real estate man, was impoverished by the northern California land boom and when he died the home was broken up. Then Grace undertook the study of water color in the studio of Julie Helen Heyman, at the same time teaching a water color class for children.

It was in this environment that she met Arthur Putnam, a struggling young sculptor of great talent, dynamic personality, and handsome physique. Grace was both pretty and talented, and it was not long before the young people were madly in love with each other. They were married in July, 1900, when Grace was twenty-two and Arthur was twenty-eight.

Quite penniless, they faced the future together with courage and optimism, and with confidence in Arthur's future as a sculptor. Perhaps it was well that they could not see how few creative years were to be allowed Arthur Putnam, for the end of his artistic career reads almost like Greek tragedy.

"Babes in the woods," their artist friends called them when with little or no money, a few weeks after their wedding, looking for inexpensive lodgings, they appeared at the Art Students' League. Arthur's former teacher sent them to an old French hotel across the way, in which Robert Louis Stevenson used to stay. But even this frugal shelter was too much for the Putnams' slender resources and we find them next occupying a single room in the same building as the Art Students' League while Arthur supported them by all sorts of odd jobs, even splitting kindling for fellow artists and stretching canvases for them. Meanwhile, pursuing his sculpture, he was regarded as a coming man.

When their first child was to be born, they moved to a cottage in Berkeley and the little one, which proved to be a girl, was named Bruce for Bruce Porter, an artist friend who had done much for them.

Commuting, in addition to his sculpture and the outside work necessary to earn a living, proved too much for Arthur and they soon moved back to San Francisco—this time occupying two rooms on the roof of a building on Washington Street—an arrangement which today would be called a penthouse. Among those, later to become famous, who had studios opening onto their roof-top were Jack London, Gelett Burgess and the Irwins.

Nobody who came in contact with this supremely happy and fascinating pair could help but love them and want to do something for them. Two friends built a play pen for the tiny Bruce in a sheltered spot among the chimneys and another gave them a perambulator with which the young father or mother took the baby for long rides across the flat roof-tops. Everybody admired Grace for the selfless way in which she had given up her own career to further that of her husband, and the cheerfulness with which she lived in all sorts of quarters without conveniences, often without necessities.

The years from 1901 to 1905 brought more work and growing reputation to Arthur Putnam and his friends continually urged a period of study in Europe. Through the good offices of Bruce Porter, Mrs. William R. Crocker offered to advance the money for the trip and take payment in work.

Leaving their small daughter Bruce with her grandmother in Portland, Oregon, and accompanied by an artist friend, they sailed for Europe. They settled down in Rome, facing the Borghese Gardens, in what had been an old monastery. Six months were spent there while Arthur studied bronze casting and prepared several things for the Salon. His animal casts attracted favorable attention and several were sold.

They spent some time in Paris and then, eighteen months after going to Europe, they joyfully turned toward home. They stopped for ten days in New York where the sculptor, Gutzon Borglum, urged Arthur to remain—even offering to share his New York studio with him should Arthur accept. But true Californians, they wanted only to get back to San Francisco.

The rebuilding of that earthquake-devastated city was under way and soon Arthur had more work than he could comfortably handle. Prosperity at length smiled on him. The high point of his recognition was indubitably the purchase of one of his bronzes, the Snarling Jaguar, by the Metropolitan Museum of Art in New York.

Meantime he had bought a lot on the lonely sea beach at the end of Golden Gate Park, and here they lived, like many other homeless San Franciscans, in a huge tent until Arthur, with his own hands, built them a small house. Later, he built a bronze casting-furnace near by. Its isolation made it an ideal location for Arthur to work without interruptions but its distance from friends and all recreation were hard for Grace although she bore it uncomplainingly.

During the years between their return from Europe in 1907, and 1910, Arthur Putnam worked prodigiously and accomplished as much, or more, than some men would have in a lifetime. But toward the end of this period, a change came over the character and personality of the artist. He who had been so abstemious began to drink heavily. Always so affectionate and tender with his wife, he became censorious and critical of her. Perhaps it was the effect of prosperity on one who had had such a hard struggle to achieve it, but more likely it was the result of the yet unrecognized brain disease which was shortly to end Arthur Putnam's career as a sculptor. Grace was bewildered and distressed by his strange attitude. There was a brief recurrence of his old affection and tenderness after the birth of their son George late in 1910, but it was of short duration.

It was not until September, 1911, that he himself began to realize his physical condition. The knowledge was forced upon him by intermittent spells of temporary paralysis of his arm. He was found on the street in an unconscious condition and rushed to the hospital. The doctors operated, removing a tumor from his brain as well as part of the brain tissue. They had little hope for his recovery, but his strong constitution asserted itself. Arthur Putnam, the physical man, lived for twenty years longer but Arthur Putnam, the sculptor, died on the operating table. When he returned from the hospital, it was as a helpless cripple. His left arm and leg were entirely paralyzed.

What a tragedy for a man, barely thirty-eight, at the height of his artistic career and just beginning to achieve fame and fortune, to be stricken thus! What frustration to be so helpless when he would have done so much!

It was small wonder that he alternated between periods of dark brooding and bitter rages that usually ended in an unconscious state. Small wonder that he turned against all his friends, his doctors, and even his faithful wife.

Grace Storey Putnam, with a nurse, took care of him; finally she dismissed the nurse to save expense. They were in the lonely beach house and his doctors feared for her life. After nearly a year, they finally persuaded her to go to New York to try to sell some of his bronzes and casts. With this plan Arthur quickly fell in, so, reluctantly, she acquiesced and his mother and sister took turns staying with him.

Grace remained in New York for some months, receiving reports from home. Then, out of a clear sky, came service of divorce papers. She rushed back to California and went with her children to the house on the beach. Arthur received her kindly but a few days later his obsession with divorcing her returned. The children were terrified by his violent rages and his unconscious seizures. The doctors warned her, again and again, on no account to remain with him in the house without a male nurse or attendant. Anxiety for her children and her ailing husband brought her close to a nervous breakdown. She finally realized the hopelessness of it all, and allowed him an uncontested divorce.

As the years went by, Arthur Putnam's mental condition improved, he grew calmer, and in 1917 he married a newspaper woman. They later went to Europe, where he stayed until the end of his life.

Meanwhile Grace Storey Putnam was faced with the problem of making a living for her young children. She felt that she did not have enough art training. Invited to stay with her brother near Berkeley, she studied for a year at the California School of Arts and Crafts, then entered the Summer School of the University of California and became a special student in the art department. This extra training enabled her to qualify to teach art for two years at Mills College.

Planning for the future, she had in mind a project of creating a doll, an infant about three days old. To this end she studied babies everywhere, in private homes, hospitals, orphanages, making sketches here and there but never seeming to find the right baby for her purpose. A neighbor suggested a visit to the Salvation Army Home. Here she found many babies, but still not the one she envisioned. Finally, one day she was called to the home to see a new baby, a little girl born out of wedlock three days before. As the blanket was removed from its face, her heart leaped—here, at last, was the baby of which she had been dreaming. This was her day off from teaching and she quickly went home for her modelling clay. The baby slept for two hours and two thirds of her mask was done when she left. She returned three days later to find to her dismay that the baby's appearance had completely changed and she could use only the back of its head and ears for the model. The rest of the face had to be done from memory.

When the heavy mold was dry, she cast several plaster heads from it. Then her brother, who was skilled at the work, cast a wax head which was painted in oils. When a soft body was added and it was dressed in baby clothes, it was remarkably like a real baby.

Giving herself six months to market the doll, Grace Storey Putnam went with her children to New York. A small loan from a friend enabled them to live but all did not go smoothly. The baby was too realistic to please the doll makers to whom it was shown. Her first idea was to have a rubber doll made, similar to the beautiful rubber dolls that came out later. The U. S. Rubber Company considered the project for some time but finally rejected it on the grounds that they were cutting down their toy production.

Finally, she showed it at Schwartz Toy Store, and Mr. Schwartz suggested that she go to George Borgfeldt and Company, who were large importers and manufacturers of toys. She had somehow missed this company, which had brought out Rose O'Neill's Kewpies.

At Borgfeldt's she first had to interview the lawyer who passed on all new undertakings. As she drew the wax baby from the bag in which she carried it, the lawyer fairly leaped for it.

"It's wonderful!" he exclaimed. "I *know* how wonderful it is, because I have a three-day-old baby just now in my own home."

He took her to the president of the company and it was agreed to sign her up to a ten-year contract.

The plaster models were sent to Germany to be cast in bisque. There were still delays and difficulties in the way, however, and it was two years from the time the contract was signed until the doll came on the market in 1920. During this time, Grace was often in financial straits. Mrs. Emma C. Clear, of the Humpty Dumpty Doll Hospital, relates an amusing story told her by Mrs. Putnam:

"Needing funds, she applied to Borgfeldt's for an advance on royalties. The Borgfeldt man was adamant. Borgfeldt always lived up to their contracts and expected other people to do the same. But she was persistent, so they called the manager. He told her the same thing, ending by calling a conference. They discussed the pros and cons. She would duck into the conference, then go back to the salesroom where the salesman was booking the buyers for her doll, then return to the conference.

"They finally gave in and one of the men asked: 'How much money do you have to have?' 'Let me see,' she said reflectively, 'my rent is due and I have to buy some groceries. I guess fifteen dollars will do.' She said he nearly choked and there was not a straight face in the place.

"When she went back to the salesroom, the salesman asked, 'Did you get the advance?' 'Yes.' 'How much?' She told him, and he also had a good laugh. 'I thought you would ask for at least three thousand dollars! Any of us would have loaned you fifteen.'"

When the Bye-lo Baby came on the market, its success was immediate. The newspapers called it "The Million Dollar Baby." That first Christmas people stood in line to buy it. Borgfeldts could not get the

Grace Storey at the time of her marriage to Arthur Putnam, sculptor

bisque heads over from Germany in time to meet the unexpected demand.

The success of her doll brought Grace Storey Putnam from real poverty to considerable prosperity until the depression caused the bottom to drop out of the doll market.

She lived in New Jersey with her brother and later in New York City while she was trying to market the doll. Upon success she took her son and daughter to Europe in 1925, then bought a home and built a studio at Sag Harbor, New York.

In 1926, she married Eugene Morahan, a well-known sculptor. In her first marriage, Grace had given up her career. It was otherwise in this second marriage. She had been on her own too long to do so this time. Artistic temperaments clashed, and although she and Eugene Morahan were fond of each other, they quarrelled, separated, and finally were divorced for a short period. Five years before her death they were reconciled and remarried.

Besides the Bye-lo Baby, Grace also created a doll house and a miniature American family to go in it, but because of the depression, and later, the Second World War, this never was produced commercially. After Mrs. Putnam's death, the original doll house and models were given to the Charles W. Bowers Memorial Museum, Santa Ana, California, where she had wished it to go.

Mrs. Emma C. Clear was an enthusiastic admirer and friend of Mrs. Putnam and one could hardly do better than to quote what Mrs. Clear says of her in a personal letter to this author:

"You asked about Mrs. Putnam . . . Her death was a surprise and a great shock. She had had an operation a year or two before and made a good recovery. She and her former husband, Gene Morahan, who was also a sculptor, had a reconciliation about five years ago. They were living on the ocean front some miles north of Santa Monica, in little home-made buildings such as artists make to their liking. She was very happy and active. They were putting in trees and shrubs, and she was writing a book.

"Shortly before that we were hearing reports of her death. She laughed about that. Her correspondence was too heavy. If she was ever to finish the book, she had to stop writing letters. So she stopped very suddenly. Knowing of her hospitalization, they decided she had died

Grace Storey Putnam with the original model of the Bye-lo Baby

An original model of Grace Storey Putnam's American family doll house with
miniature furniture by Eugene Morahan
Courtesy of Charles W. Bowers Memorial Museum, Santa Ana, California

when she did not answer her letters. But she was very much alive and
worrying about me when I was ill . . .

"She was most interesting when you had her alone but she was shy
and a poor speaker when talking to a group. She was guest speaker at one
of the Santa Ana receptions and it really fell flat. She told me afterwards
that she never was so embarrassed in her life. She knew she would be a
failure, but she was fond of Mrs. Coulter and Mrs. Coulter was so in-
sistent.

"It is funny what a small world it is. Some years ago, before I met
Mrs. Putnam, a lady brought in a Putnam Bye-lo Baby for eye work. The
Baby had a note on it and Mrs. Putnam's autograph in ink. I asked the
lady about it. Mrs. Putnam had been a neighbor of hers in a suburb of
New York City. She and George, her little son, were living in a chicken
house which Grace had remodelled into a comfortable little home.
George and her son were chums and the son happened to mention that
it was his mother's birthday. The first of the Bye-lo heads had just come
from Germany. Mrs. Putnam had given her this doll for a birthday
present.

"It was during this chicken house period, George Putnam recalls,
that he, a young boy, planted a garden; but for some reason he planted
only beets. That fall he went away to school and his mother, to stretch

48

Grace Storey Putnam and her son, George

her limited resources, ate every beet—every single beet—in the garden, tops and all. Somehow she never cared for beets afterwards.

"She spent one weekend with us, before her marriage to Mr. Morahan. I tried my best to get her to join our staff. She needed the money badly and our pay was good. She said she could not sell her art. She could do any kind of a war job on a time basis, but not art work. When the spirit moved, she could work twenty-four hours at a stretch. We had a vacant room but she preferred the trailer which she had built for herself.

"She showed me her latest model, a lovely young girl reclining on a bench. It is beautiful—the body she left for me to design . . . She also gave me the last wee bisque Bye-lo Baby she had. I told her that I was not collecting and would not keep it. I kept it on my desk for about a year and enjoyed it. Then when I had ceased to see it and was afraid it might get broken, I sold it and sent her the check.

"She was a precious person and we all miss her."

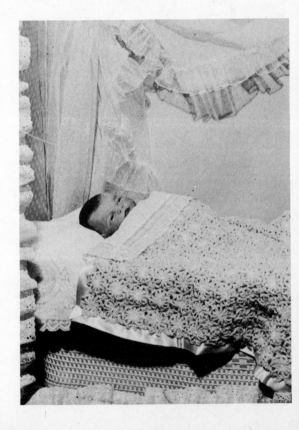

Above,
Grace Storey Putnam's daughter, Bruce,
   now Mrs. K. C. Walkey

Right,
Wax model of Grace Storey Putnam's
   Bye-lo Baby

Courtesy of Charles W. Bowers Memorial Museum, Santa Ana, California

5

Japanese Festival Dolls

IN Japan, March 3, the Festival of the Dolls, is the girls' special day of all the year. It is sometimes called "The Peach Blossom Festival," although it is a month ahead of the peach blossom season, with which it used to coincide under the old lunar calendar. Now, the term "Plum Blossom Festival" would be more fitting, but the pale pink of the peach blossom symbolizes maidenhood, so the old name is still used. Japanese festival dolls are not toys to be played with, but family heirlooms handed down from generation to generation for perhaps hundreds of years. They are ceremonial dolls and are treated with profound respect. They are only on display during this one month of the year. The other eleven they sleep peacefully in the family godown, a fireproof building of brick and iron which every wealthy and noble family has built a safe distance from the house to protect the family treasures from fire and theft. Japanese houses are built of highly inflammable wood, have paper screens and straw mats, and are liable to go up in smoke at the first spark.

The Doll Festival has a known history of a thousand years, but back of that, its origins are shrouded in the mists of the legendary past. It may be that the Doll Festival had its beginning as an act of worship for the Emperor who was believed to be of divine ancestry, "The Son of Heaven." For many hundred years, during the rule of the powerful shoguns, the Emperor and Empress were kept secluded in their palace surrounded by certain lords and ladies who shared their seclusion. The

51

multitude, who never looked on the face of their Emperor, showed their reverence and loyalty for him by the ceremonial of the Doll Festival, which represents the imperial household in miniature; the Emperor and Empress, their lords and ladies, ministers of state, ladies in waiting, musicians and soldiers, who surrounded them in the palace. A set of these ceremonial dolls will consist of at least fifteen and may run into hundreds.

About ten days before March 3, the mother and daughters begin to make preparations for the Doll Festival, in a special room or alcove of the house. There they set up five or seven steps covered with crimson damask. They arrange the dolls on these steps, surrounded by traditional properties consisting of all manner of miniature furniture and dishes for sweetmeats.

On the topmost shelf, before a folding golden screen, are placed the Emperor and Empress, he on the left, she on the right. They are sumptuously clad in robes of state of the olden time which are not unlike those worn today on certain ceremonial occasions. The Emperor holds a wooden sceptre and wears on his head the old style Japanese crown. The Empress wears a Chinese style crown with metal ornaments hanging down from it. At each end of the shelf is placed a lantern, and a ceremonial tray is in the center of the shelf. Sometimes tiny dogs, symbolizing faithfulness and honor, are placed on the shelf.

On the next shelf below the royal pair are three maids of honor, represented as ready to serve sake. On the next shelf below the maids of honor are placed two imperial guardsmen, and below them are five musicians with varied musical instruments. On the ends of the lowest step are placed two small artificial blooming trees, a mandarin orange and a cherry tree. In spaces between the dolls are placed all manner of miniature furniture and lacquered dishes to delight the heart of the little housewife, and lozenge-shaped trays holding rice cakes. From the ceiling, suspended by silken cords, are two tight balls of orange blossoms and cherry blossoms.

Other items such as a ceremonial oxcart and a palanquin of the old times are sometimes added to the display. The palanquin was not used by the imperial family but by the court ladies and some officials. As stated before, a set of ceremonial dolls may consist of a minimum of fifteen or may run into hundreds—ministers of state, shoguns (traditional Japanese warlords), diamyos (lords), dancing girls and entertainers.

A ferocious shogun on the left and on the right, an armored warrior on horseback
near the symbolic pine tree
Collection of Miss Elizabeth MacMahon, Everett, Massachusetts

Japanese Emperor and Empress dolls about eleven inches high and reputedly two
hundred years old
Collection of Miss Elizabeth MacMahon, Everett, Massachusetts

A bride usually takes her set of dolls to her new home, and when a
daughter is born, she often buys a new set of dolls for the infant, while
relatives and friends also give dolls to the newborn. These dolls are highly
prized by Japanese families and it is a real tragedy for them when they
are lost through fire or earthquake.

When at length the great day dawns, friends and relatives call on the
little girls to congratulate them on the excellence of their arrangement,
and little girls go to see each other's displays. Sake, a thick white sweet
wine of about the alcoholic content of beer, together with rice cakes and
sweetmeats are served as refreshments to the guests, after first being
proffered to the Emperor and Empress and then to the other dolls. Even
the children are given small cups of sake.

The Doll Festival, besides being a means of showing parents' affection
for their children—and it is a strong quality of Japanese character—
teaches, and is intended to teach, loyalty to their Emperor, a sense of the
continuity of their government, love and respect for their parents. Much
of its meaning can be traced back to ancestor worship which, like
Buddhism, came across from the mainland of China in the remote periods
of time.

54

Warlord with ladies of the court. Note the lovely hairdos of these fine dolls
Collection of Miss Elizabeth MacMahon, Everett, Massachusetts

While legend has it that the first doll was made in Japan two thousand years ago, the first known representation of dolls in genre paintings is in a book of pictures published in the second year of the Tokagura period, 1672. In this picture, two dolls are shown dancing as puppets. (Puppet shows seem to have been an early form of Japanese recreation.)

A child's book of pictures, whose Japanese title translates *Moral Pictures for Children*, shows two doll makers at work. This picture is analogous to the ancient German pictures of doll makers in Max von Bohn's *Dolls and Puppets*.

French scientists studying Japanese culture and history—such men as Professors Blaringham and Maspero—have called antique Japanese dolls "genre paintings in three dimensions." They meant by this that the Japanese prints and genre paintings which were so popular in both Europe and America before World War I, showed the Japanese customs, habits, civilization, and costumes in two dimensions. The dolls,

55

however, they considered much more valuable since they offered a three-dimensional view of the figures. This, too, is comparable to the way in which Western doll collectors find their old dolls—when in original condition and costumes—lessons in civilization, social customs and costumes of the times from which the dolls come down.

The old festival dolls were seldom to be bought in Japan, but since World War II, many have, for one reason or another, come on the market.

One of the fortunate ones who has been able to acquire a collection is Miss Elizabeth MacMahon of Everett, Massachusetts, a member of Doll Collectors of America and a high school instructor at Everett. A former high school associate of Miss MacMahon held a government position during two years of the United States occupation of Japan and was able to act as Miss MacMahon's emissary in getting together a really outstanding collection of the old dolls and accessories.

Miniature traveling shrine of gold and black lacquer, an ox and palanquin and on
the right, a boy on a hobby horse
Collection of Miss Elizabeth MacMahon, Everett, Massachusetts

6

Dolls with a History

FIRST PART

DOLLS IN VERMONT HISTORICAL SOCIETY MUSEUM

TO the Vermonters who experienced it, the great flood of November 2, 1927, stands second only to the deluge of Noah. Several days of torrential rains which could not be absorbed by the frozen ground swelled the tributaries of the White River and the Connecticut River to unprecedented heights and caused up-state power dams to give way, creating the greatest flood in the history of the state. The writer, who came to Vermont the following January, recalls seeing grass and other debris still caught in the trees along Route No. 4, at a height of ten or twelve feet above the highway, below which the bed of the river lay many, many feet. Fortunately, there were few human casualties, but there was much property damage.

In the Vermont Historical Society Museum at Montpelier, Vermont, the oldest of the four old dolls that had been gifts to the Society was swept away. The doll was afterwards found in the debris but was greatly damaged and all trace of her history, and data concerning her, was lost. She is now known simply as "the doll that went through the Great Flood." The doll is obviously of the Empire Period, or about 1820.

She is approximately fourteen inches tall. Her head and body are molded in plaster of Paris over a wooden core. Nothing remains of her legs, which probably were washed away by the waters of the flood, except two slender rough sticks of wood—doubtless the foundation. The head is smooth and egg-shaped, similar to the 1820 English wax dolls, most of which have their hair set in slits in their heads. (See the author's *The Dolls of Yesterday.*) The Vermont doll's head has the remains of a wig, into which are woven strands of heavy gold cord and pearl beads. The egg-shaped head, six inches in circumference and two inches high, is perfectly smooth with the features painted on a thin masque of papier-mâché. The only feature that stands out is the nose. The painted eyes are rather large and definitely turned to the right. The arms have no hands, and apparently never did have. The forearms are small, tight rolls of homespun linen. What the feet may have been we can only guess, of course.

Here is a case in which the clothing helps to determine the age of the doll. The dress is Empire of plain gray taffeta, with a half-inch puff around the bottom of the long narrow skirt. The décolletage is finished with silver braid and there are the remains of a guimpe. The petticoat is of plain homespun linen.

There are two dolls of the milliner's model type in the Historical Society's collection. One is from the Lizzie Langdon Estate and is nineteen and three-quarters inches tall.

The second, known as "the Aldus Knight doll," was given by one Aldus Knight to his niece in 1853. The doll, however, by her hairdress, seems to be of an earlier date—about 1845.

The fourth doll, which is only loaned to the Society, is Nelly Gray, a more modern doll which belonged to the late wife of ex-Governor Weeks of Vermont. The head is a replacement.

CANFIELD DOLLS

Through the courtesy of the author, Mrs. Dorothy Canfield Fisher, of Arlington, Vermont, we are able to show a picture of the Canfield family dolls of Vermont. Mrs. Canfield Fisher has no special interest in dolls, as such, but regards these as worthy of being handed on to future generations.

The photograph was taken by Mr. Herbert Wheaton Condon whose book, *Old Vermont Houses*, is known to lovers of architecture everywhere.

Doll that went through the Great Flood
Collection of Vermont Historical Society Museum, Montpelier, Vermont

Aldus Knight doll
Collection of Vermont Historical Society Museum, Montpelier, Vermont

Left, Doll from the Lizzie Langdon estate

Right, "Nelly Gray" who belonged to the wife of Ex-Governor Weeks
Both are from the collection of Vermont Historical Society Museum,
  Montpelier, Vermont

TWO MYSTERY DOLLS

Two mystery dolls, similar to "Sarah Swan Miles" in *The Dolls of
Yesterday,* are owned by Miss Blanche L. Masciotte of Medfield, Massachusetts. They are in wonderful condition and their original handmade
clothing of old prints is a delight to their owner who is the head of the
Peabody High School, an endowed school for the teaching of the
domestic arts.

The larger of the two dolls has been in Miss Masciotte's possession
for more than thirty years. The smaller, a more recent acquisition, had
been in the same family eighty years, according to a note found on the
doll. The reverse side of the note said: "Dressed by Josephine Meissinger
who married a Carney of Falboro, Massachusetts. She is buried in the
Balboro cemetery."

MELISSA ANN ALBEE

Old dolls are where you find them—and that may be anywhere, but
certainly the maternity floor of the Mary Hitchcock Memorial Hospital

Dolls of the Canfield family of Vermont
Courtesy of Mrs. Dorothy Canfield Fisher

at Hanover, New Hampshire, would seem the most unlikely of all places.

On our way there for an operation, late one Saturday afternoon, Mr. Al Mills, in charge of the ambulance, said jokingly, "Do you know where they told me to put you? On the maternity floor." I thought he was joking, because that didn't seem the logical place for me, but sure enough, that was where we landed, the hospital being much overcrowded.

Convalescing, one of our visitors was Mrs. Laura Murray, widow of a Dartmouth College professor. Knowing our fondness for old dolls, she brought with her to amuse us, an old doll that had belonged to her aunt, Miss Melissa Ann Albee, a school teacher in her home town of Lawrence, Massachusetts, a generation ago. Before she left, we had persuaded her to let us buy the doll to add to our collection.

A most fascinating creature, Melissa Ann, named for her first mistress, is a ten-inch version of the usual type of brown-eyed china doll which dates from 1841 and which was given to Mrs. Murray's aunt in 1861, when she was ten years old. Her hair is arranged behind her ears, and she wears her original costume.

1

2

1. "Melissa Ann Albee"—brown-eyed
   china doll
St. George Collection

2. Two mystery dolls
Collection of Blanche L. Masciotte,
   Medfield, Massachusetts

3. "Ann Kennedy"—1863
St. George Collection

3

Melissa Ann Albee, the owner, kept house for her father until his death and taught school in her native town of Lawrence, Massachusetts. In her later years she travelled much between east and west, as her brothers and sisters lived in Iowa.

It is dolls such as this which have a definite history, that help us to place the periods in which certain types of dolls were made.

Going home in the ambulance, I flashed the doll on Mr. Mills, saying: "You see, I did not go to the maternity ward for nothing!"

"A woman will always have the last word," he said.

ANN KENNEDY, 1863

Ann was bought for Flora Ann Kennedy of Bridgewater, Vermont in 1863 when her little mistress was eight years old. The dainty old hand-made clothing which she wears is all original. The body is fourteen inches tall and the china head is of fine quality and great beauty.

Ann has been preserved through these many years by Flora Kennedy's daughter, Mrs. Sadie Perkins Fraser of West Hartford, Vermont, and formerly of Woodstock, Vermont, who herself had played with the doll. Mrs. Fraser, who has steadfastly refused offers for the doll from many collectors, finally let her come to the author's collection, feeling that here Ann would find permanent preservation.

MR. SHAKESPEARE ON HIS HONEYMOON

Tasha Tudor, the illustrator, who in private life is Mrs. Thomas McCready, Jr., of Contacook, New Hampshire, created Mr. Shakespeare in December of 1950 as a Christmas gift for her children and as a "husband" for her porcelain-headed French fashion doll, "Sethany Ann." Sethany Ann's elaborate French wardrobe bears the labels of Mlle. Calixto Huret, who lived in Paris in 1850. However, her Anderson gingham going-away gown and her hat were fashioned by Mrs. McCready, herself a student of costume. "Nicey Melinda," an 1830 English doll of papier-mâché, notable for her deep blue, unthreaded glass eyes, was bridesmaid. Tasha Tudor's flair for imaginative detail shows up in the tiny gold wedding ring on the third finger of the bride's kid hand. These two old dolls are the heroines of Tasha Tudor's book, *The Dolls' Christmas.**

* Published in 1950 by Oxford University Press, Inc., New York.

Left to right, Sethany Ann, Mr. Shakespeare, Nicey Melinda
Collection of Mrs. Thomas McCready, Jr., Contacook, New Hampshire

DOLL FROM ALASKA

A doll that is a souvenir of World War II is the wooden Eskimauan

65

Left, Alaskan doll of World War II
Collection of Mrs. Mark Powers, West Lebanon, New Hampshire

Right, Dolls of World War II from Luzon
Collection of Mrs. Grace Toalson, Osceola, Missouri

doll brought from Alaska by Norman Powers of White River Junction, Vermont, to his mother. The doll is about eight inches tall, carved from a flat piece of wood, and its clothing is a combination of various bits of fine fur. The trader from whom he bought it came from Bethel, Alaska, and the doll was made by the natives of the Kuskokwim River Valley.

Another historic doll of the Far North was that made for Commodore Robert E. Peary's wee daughter who was born on the North Pole voyage of discovery. She was the first white child to be born north of the Arctic circle. The Eskimos, who had never seen a white baby before, were devoted to the tiny Marie Ahnighito and they made for her a doll very similar to Mrs. Mark Powers' doll. Mrs. Peary, the widow of Commodore Peary, who now lives in Portland, Maine, does not remember what became of the doll. Back in 1903, Mrs. Peary published two charming books about her little daughter, the first of which was called *The Snow Baby*.

DOLLS FROM LUZON

These two dolls from the Philippine jungles have no duplicates and "money would not buy them," writes Mrs. Grace Toalson of Osceola, Missouri. Surely their story is worthy of a place among "Dolls with a History."

"During World War II," says Mrs. Toalson, "my son, an infantry major, was in the Northern Luzon campaign. A lot of his work was with the guerillas. While the war was going on, two dolls were made for me by a guerilla woman. The woman doll is especially nice, I think—but the man is nice too. The hair wigs are from the maker's own head. She has embroidered the Oriental features onto the faces. Costumes are correct. The poverty of the people during that period shows in the doll bodies where tiny pieces of cloth are pieced together to make them. She had asked my son if he could furnish material, but that he could not do—didn't have it, of course.

"The man's trousers are made of small scraps pieced together. Some of the seams are visible in the picture. His coat is of beautiful material. Their small bodies are pitiful with all the piecing together of small bits of material."

JAPANESE DOLL SURRENDERED IN WORLD WAR II

When the Japanese submarine 1-401, one of the two largest subs afloat at the time, surrendered to the U.S.S. Sequando, Commander Spruance in command, without a shot being fired, one of the objects passed over formally in the surrender was a Japanese doll, the mascot of the Japanese sailors. It is now owned by Mrs. Mattie Walker of San Diego, California.

The full story of the surrender of the great submarine is told in the newspaper of the submarine base, February 6, 1946.

"The U.S.S. Sequando, with Commander Spruance in command, upon making contact with the Japanese submarine 1-401, found her skipper willing to surrender; however, in order to save face, the Japanese in command would not allow any officer to board her. The Sequando's executive officer then donned the uniform of an enlisted man and boarded the 1-401 in charge of the prize crew.

"Before any American set foot on the deck of the submarine, the

Japanese Division Captain committed hari-kari, and was thrown into the sea on the lee side of the submarine; and thus was not seen by any American. During this time the 1-401 broke radio silence to establish the fact that she was surrendering and was immediately upbraided by the Japanese naval officials.

"The prize crew of forty men and three officers took command, after a colorful and fastidious ceremony at which the Japanese presented a doll and four quarts of beer to Commander Spruance. The Japanese commander asked for permission to keep his sword. This request was granted with the understanding that it would not be used to commit hari-kari.

"Commander Spruance's first intention was to take the 1-401 into Tokyo, but to have her berthed there would have been a great disgrace to her officers; consequently it was decided that she should be taken into the Yokoluska Naval Base.

"Along with his crew Commander Nabu was kept aboard for three weeks; in this time the Japanese were to clean the submarine so that the Americans could live on her. First, the 1-401 stores, which consisted mainly of sake (not unlike our beer), polished and unpolished rice, dried octopus and wine, were thrown overboard. This was followed by an inspection of the crew's gear topside; it was found to be in a very deplorable condition. One man had almost identical gear to that of the next. Almost every one had some type of foodstuffs in his possession on which he intended to subsist when he should be discharged from the submarine and the Japanese Navy. During the entire inspection the men were extremely cooperative. The boat was painted and minor repairs were effected.

"Found among the crew's gear were many Japanese-American dictionaries from which the men had endeavored to obtain a working knowledge of our language."

When, during the course of our research, the picture of the doll was submitted to an expert in Oriental matters, he reported that by her attire the doll was evidently the representation of some noted courtesan. Sailors in Japan sometimes use either a picture or image of the favorite of some famous war lord or sea hero as a mascot to bring them good luck. (The maple leaf on the doll's costume signifies "Good Luck.") Women of this class in Japan hold a position somewhat analogous to that of the hetaerae among the ancient Greeks. Up to the time it was forbidden by the Ameri-

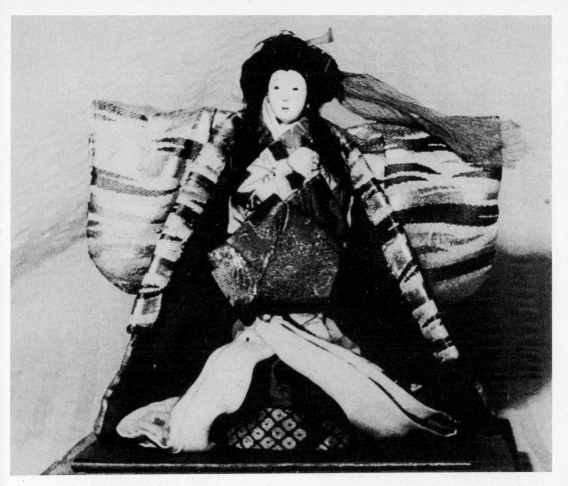

Doll surrendered with Japanese submarine 1-401 in World War II
Courtesy of Mrs. Mattie Walker, San Diego, California

can Occupation authorities, there was an annual festival or parade held in their honor.

THE FIRST DOLL EVER MADE IN BENNINGTON, VERMONT

In the earlier days of doll collecting, many collectors had what they considered doll heads made in the potteries of Bennington, Vermont, but careful investigation of the waste heaps at the Bennington potteries have since revealed no remains of doll heads. This, of course, makes it clear that Bennington potteries never made dolls since, if they had, some trace such as indestructible fragments would have remained.

In 1949, two Bennington women, Mrs. John Stone and Mrs. Norman Stratton, collaborated in the making of a doll which is a combination of Bennington clay, wood flour and other materials. Molds of lastex had been made over old china doll heads. The dolls are not baked as china dolls are but allowed to dry for about three weeks and then painted with enamel. The materials used still vary somewhat as the dolls are in the experimental stage and Mesdames Stone and Stratton are trying to overcome what they consider to be the most serious fault—the heaviness of the heads.

The first completed doll was given to the Bennington Museum. In accepting it, John Spargo, the curator, who is the greatest living authority on Bennington ware, claimed, "This is the first doll head ever made in Bennington."

Stone-Stratton doll
Collection of Bennington Museum, Bennington, Vermont

Dolls with a History

SECOND PART

ONE of the finest collections of dolls in the United States and one that contains more than the usual number of historic dolls is that of Mrs. Imogene Anderson of New York City. Photographs of two outstanding dolls from the collection have been loaned by Mrs. Anderson for this book. One of these is an unusual wax Jenny Lind. Most of the Jenny Lind dolls, which were made in 1850 when "the Swedish Nightingale," as she was popularly known, made her first concert tour in the United States under the management of P. T. Barnum, are china and have black hair. The wax Jenny Lind is unique because it has golden hair, as the real Jenny Lind had.

The doll is about twelve inches tall, hollow, and is made of wax. Its features, hair and boots are painted on. She is dressed in pink mull with a full skirt trimmed in narrow white silk braid and has on a complete set of underclothes. Her hat is straw with white rosettes under each ear.

Mrs. Anderson bought the doll from a woman in upper New York State. It was contained in a white moire box.

"Old as it is," says Mrs. Anderson, "it is one of the most beautiful dolls I have ever seen."

In the same collection is "Georgiana White," which belonged to a direct descendant of Peregrine White, one of the pilgrims on the Mayflower. Documented and authenticated, her photograph is from the Plymouth Society. Brought from France about 1862, she has a porcelain head that turns on a kid body; she is about eighteen inches tall. The patentee's name, Mme. Rojomer of Paris, is stamped on the doll's kid chest. She has porcelain arms and legs, beautifully molded feet with low-cut white kid shoes with heels, violet-blue eyes and a light brown hair wig with a waterfall hairdo in a silken net.

She carries her white silk bonnet and is dressed in white mull with rosettes of ribbon and has a miniature hoop that holds out her five hand-made petticoats.

She has a very complete trousseau; her underclothes marked cross stitch; a complete set of toilet articles. Her taffeta dresses have labels. There are about six dresses with complete accessories and she has a wooden Victorian trunk with a brass plate on it marked "G. W."

OLD SUSAN

In the Museum of the City of New York are many historical dolls. One of the oldest of these, "Old Susan," is a wooden jointed doll bought in Holland in 1773 by the Reverend Benjamin Moore as a gift for Martha Buchanan. The Rev. Benjamin Moore was rector of old Trinity Church in New York in 1815.

Equally interesting is the wooden jointed doll with hair and brown glass eyes bought by Joseph King for his daughter who later married Lindley Murray, the grammarian, and re-dressed by her in 1846 for her daughter, Mary King Murray.

STIMSON DOLL

A doll of double historical significance is the lovely bride which came from France on the maiden voyage of the famous steamship, GREAT EASTERN, to the little girl who was to become the mother of Henry L. Stimson, Secretary of State during the Hoover administration.

The GREAT EASTERN was a sensation in her day, being the largest steamship ever built up to that time. Indeed, it was not until the CELTIC was completed in England in 1901 that her size was ever equalled. In 1852 the directors of the steamship company met and decided that because of the expense of maintaining coaling stations along the trans-Atlantic route, it would be expedient to build a ship of such size that it could carry its own fuel for the voyage to and fro across the

Blonde-haired Jenny Lind of wax
Collection of Mrs. Imogene Anderson, New York, New York

1

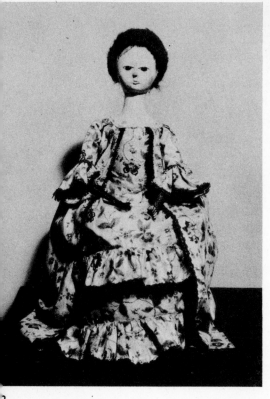

2

3

1. "Georgiana White"—French fashion doll with porcelain head
Collection of Mrs. Imogene Anderson, New York, New York

2. "Old Susan," wooden doll bought in Holland in 1773 by the Reverend Benjamin Moore
Collection of Museum of the City of New York, New York, N. Y.

3. Wooden doll from Holland bought in 1805 by Joseph King for his daughter
Collection of Museum of the City of New York, New York, N. Y.

4. Doll brought over on the maiden voyage of the GREAT EASTERN to the little girl who later became the mother of Henry L. Stimson
Collection of Museum of the City of New York, New York, N. Y.

4

Atlantic; so the GREAT EASTERN was planned to carry one thousand passengers, five thousand tons of merchandise and fifteen thousand tons of coal. She was to be 692 feet in length, 82 feet in breadth. She had both paddle wheels and a screw propeller for power.

The ship was built from 1852 to 1859, and during the building and the next twenty years, the great ship went through a series of accidents and vicissitudes hard to equal. It was never a financial success because it was built at a time when travel and business conditions did not warrant the construction of a ship so large.

Originally built for travel to Australia and the East, the directors decided to try a trial run across the Atlantic. In September of 1859 it set out from the Thames but an explosion of the steam pipes killed seven and wounded several others and the voyage ended at Weymouth. It started out again in June of 1860 and this time completed the voyage to New York. This was the trip on which the Stimson doll was brought over. The ship plied between England and the United States several times that year, then political relations between the two countries became strained and war seemed imminent; the GREAT EASTERN was transformed into a troop ship.

In 1865 and 1866 the GREAT EASTERN laid the Atlantic cable. In 1868 it again became a passenger ship to carry passengers for the Paris Exposition. Again the venture was not a financial success.

In 1868 it returned to cable laying and laid many important cables in the Atlantic and in the Mediterranean and the Red Sea. The ship was broken up in 1879.

SANITARY FAIR DOLLS

A charming ten-inch china pair, a bride and groom, was dressed for the Brooklyn Sanitary Fair in 1864.

The Brooklyn and Long Island Sanitary Fair, to give it its full official title, was one of a series of such fairs held for the benefit of the United States Sanitary Commission which was providing medicines and comforts for the soldiers in Civil War hospitals. They were held in the principal cities of the United States and some of the lesser cities, too. The first one was held in Lowell, Massachusetts, and opened January 24, 1864. The Brooklyn Sanitary Fair opened February 24, 1864.

A contemporary account says of the doll booth: "The Old Woman in the Shoe stood not far from here. It was not, as might at first appear, the idea of the Hide and Leather Committee; but it originated with a lady from one of the city churches. The Old Woman was represented by a child of tender years dressed in mob cap and spectacles; established in a huge shoe and having so many dolls she really did not know what to do. She sold them, however, for about four hours in succession, when she was relieved by another little girl and by still another in turn."

The largest and most successful of the Sanitary Fairs was that of Philadelphia. The first steps toward a Sanitary Fair in Philadelphia were taken on January 8, 1864, and the fair opened June 8 and closed June 28. Over a million and thirty-five thousand dollars was raised for the United States Sanitary Commission by the Philadelphia Fair.

No building in the city was large enough to contain the Fair as planned so a special structure was called for in Union Square. Two million feet of lumber were laid down in the Square and in just forty days the structure was completed.

In 1857, William Allen Butler had written a poem, "Nothing to Wear," which was much admired during the Civil War days. It ran in part, thus:

"Miss Flora McFlimsey, of Madison Square,
Has made three separate journeys to Paris;
And her father assures me, each time she was there,
That she and her friend, Mrs. Harris,
Spent six consecutive weeks, without stopping,
In one continuous round of shopping;
Shopping alone, and shopping together,
At all hours of the day, and in all sorts of weather,
For all manner of things that a woman can put
On the crown of her head, or the sole of her foot,
Or wrap round her shoulders, or fit round her waist,
Or that can be sewed on, or pinned on, or laced,
Or tied on with a string, or stitched on with a bow,
In front or behind, above or below;
For bonnets, mantillas, capes, collars, and shawls;
Dresses for breakfasts, and dinners, and balls,

Dresses to sit in and walk in, and stand in;
Dresses to dance in, and flirt in, and talk in,
Dresses in which to do nothing at all in;
Dresses for winter, spring, summer and fall
All of them different in color and pattern,
Silk, velvet and lace, crepe, velvet and satin,
Brocade and broadcloth, and other material,
Quite as expensive, and much more ethereal;
In short, for all things that could be thought of
Or milliner, modiste or tradesman be bought of
From ten-thousand-franc robes to twenty-sous frills;
In all quarters of Paris, and to every store,
While McFlimsey in vain stormed, scolded, and swore,
They footed the streets, and he footed the bills!

· · · · ·

And yet, though scarce three months have passed
    since the day
This merchandise went, on twelve carts, up Broadway,
This same Miss McFlimsey, of Madison Square,
The last time we met was in utter despair,
Because she had nothing whatever to wear!
Nothing to wear! Now, as this is a true ditty,
I do not assert this, you know, is between us—
That she is in a state of absolute nudity,
Like Powers Greek Slave, or the Medici Venus;
But I do mean to say, I have heard her declare
That she hadn't a thing in the world to wear."

A doll, illustrating this poem, was prepared for the Philadelphia Sanitary Fair by Miss Mary Kuhn of Philadelphia and was purchased by Mrs. Henry E. Drayton for the sum of $250. She was presented to the Pennsylvania Historical Society.

Probably no "fashion doll" of any time or place has ever had so large and expensive a wardrobe as the miniature "Miss Flora McFlimsey." Her dresses were donated by the most fashionable dressmakers of her time. Her bonnets were made by well-known milliners, and were of a variety for every occasion; her hand-made shoes matched her various costumes.

"Miss Flora McFlimsey of Madison Square"
Courtesy The Historical Society of Pennsylvania, Philadelphia, Pennsylvania

Even her corsets were made by Mme. Barrette. Her outfits are complete to a riding habit, skating costume, evening and daytime dresses, dressing gowns, and a large variety of underwear and nightgowns. Among her paraphernalia, you can find visiting cards, writing paper with monograms, work basket, towels, handkerchiefs, raincoat, umbrella, photograph album, and all the accessories that a lady of fashion would have had in the early 'sixties.

Not until World War I did Flora again appear in public. This was at a bazaar held under the management of the Emergency Aid, again to raise funds for the Army and Navy, as she had done in the Civil War.

After a brief period of retirement, Flora was asked again to help raise funds, this time for the restoration of the Powell House, one of the historical residences of Philadelphia. This was held under the auspices of the Philadelphia Society for Restoration of Landmarks, at John Wana-maker's store in Philadelphia, from November 5 to November 18, 1938.

During World War II, she again came out of her retirement to raise funds for various relief purposes. Flora has, therefore, done her bit in three conflicts.

Flora was presented to the Historical Society of Pennsylvania by Mrs. J. Madison Taylor, daughter of Mrs. Henry E. Drayton, on March 20, 1945.

LUCRETIA MOTT'S DOLL

Lucretia Mott, pioneer suffragist, anti-slavery advocate, and recognized preacher of the Society of Friends, was born January 23, 1793 on the island of Nantucket. Her parents were Quakers, as had been her forebears for many generations. She was descended from Tristam Coffin who emigrated from Devonshire, England, and became one of the first purchasers of the island.

On April 10, 1811, Lucretia married James Mott, a business partner of her father. Six children were born to them, five of them surviving infancy. She died November 11, 1880. Lucretia Mott's most important work was in behalf of women's rights.

The little Quaker-garbed doll, now minus an eye, was the childhood treasure of Lucretia Mott, and is now in the notable doll collection of Mrs. Edmund Poetter of Reading, Vermont, who received it directly from Mrs. Arthur Patton and Miss Elizabeth Hawes, the grand-nieces of Lucretia Mott.

THE ADVENTURES OF JEDEDIAH

Jedediah, mascot of the Churchill family, is undoubtedly the most widely traveled of American dolls, and if he is not the most cultured, it is not for lack of educational opportunities. "The Adventures of Jedediah," which were vicariously shared from his desk in a prosaic business office on Broadway by his now octogenarian owner, Arthur Churchill, for more than sixty years, read like "Gulliver's Travels."

Jedediah came into being in 1878 in Montclair, New Jersey. The occasion for his "borning" was a large church fair, New England fashion,

Left, Bride and groom dressed for the Brooklyn Sanitary Fair, 1864
Collection of Museum of the City of New York, New York, N. Y.

Right, Doll that belonged to Lucretia Mott, pioneer suffragist
Collection of Mrs. Edmund Poetter, Reading, Vermont

for which Mrs. Mercy Hubbard Starkweather, herself New England born, made and contributed a number of flannel dolls.

That fall, her sixteen year old grandson, Arthur Churchill, took one of these dolls, which he had christened "Jedediah," to boarding school, the Upton Seminary, New Preston, Connecticut. When Arthur's brother William went to Yale in 1882, he cast a possessive eye on the doll and carried him away for three years at that school, so Jedediah was well launched on his career of education and travel.

When William later went to Samoa as United States Consul General, Jedediah did not go but, instead, in the company of Edward Willys Taylor, later to become an eminent brain surgeon in Boston, Jedediah obtained a thorough medical education. After graduation from Harvard University and Harvard Medical School in 1891, he was privileged to spend two years at the Universities of Berlin and Freiburg. It was then that he acquired the antique coin purse which was owned by William Churchill, Sr., Arthur Churchill's father, and which bears a brass plate with his name.

After a brief rest in Arthur Churchill's office, and another dose of Harvard, Jedediah first became involved in man's all too frequent wars. With Clarence, Arthur Churchill's younger brother, and his mother Jedediah went to Yokohama. While in the Far East, he and Clarence served with the Shanghai Volunteers but they never saw action in the Boxer Rebellion.

While in Yokohama, Mrs. Churchill found a wife for Jedediah, all decked out in native finery. She called her Jenediah. After reaching home in Montclair, Jenediah was destined to keep the home-fire burning while her spouse traveled and adventured.

Five years later, in 1910, Jedediah was touring Europe with Miss Florence Gerrish, Arthur Churchill's niece. Then, after a quiet period of several years in the Broadway office of Arthur Churchill, he again went soldiering, this time into World War I with a niece-in-law of Arthur Churchill's who enlisted as a dietitian. With the ubiquitous Jedediah, she was active in service in France, and generously recognized his military standing by decorating him with a miniature Croix de Guerre, which he still wears.

Another generation of Churchills now took Jedediah in hand, sponsored him through Annapolis and from 1923 until 1940 shuttled him back and forth from Europe to Rutgers, Marietta, Williams, Princeton and Cornell. Apparently his fame as a scholar had been spread abroad, for the colleges were willing to accept him on a part-time basis.

During 1940 and 1941, Jedediah's naval training was put to use and he sailed with Lieutenant Commander George Kennedy on several vessels on the Atlantic and the Pacific. Then his active service was interrupted in order that his portrait might be painted by Frances Weston Hoyt of Montclair, New Jersey. This picture was accepted by the Montclair Art Association and is now in the possession of Arthur Churchill.

This year, 1941, seems to have been an important one in Jedediah's career. It was then that he joined with half a dozen other Churchills, to form a corporation to be known as The Churchills of America, Inc.

On *facing page*, "Jedediah," the Churchill family mascot, as painted by Frances Weston Hoyt
Courtesy of Mr. Arthur Churchill, Woodstock, Vermont

The sole purpose of this corporation was to give moral and financial aid to their illustrious namesake, Winston Churchill, Prime Minister of Great Britain.

Back into the Navy with Kennedy, now a Captain, Jedediah's crowning adventure occurred in the year 1945 when Japan surrendered. They were with Transport Division 105 for the invasion of Okinawa, the entry into Tokyo Bay and the occupation of Japan.

Jedediah then returned for a well-earned rest with his chief sponsor, Arthur Churchill, who meanwhile had changed his residence from Montclair to Woodstock, Vermont. The educational urge, however, possessed Jedediah once more, and together with many another GI he went off to college again. Unlike his comrades, he selected a women's college. His sponsor at Radcliffe was none other than Florence Gerrish who twice had been his traveling companion in Europe and who is now in charge of the girls' dormitories at Radcliffe. Not for long did the restless Jedediah stay put!

Late in 1948, he threw in his lot with Elizabeth Whitman who was hostess in a service club at headquarters, United States Constabulary, in the American zone of occupied Germany. It is to be noted that Elizabeth Whitman is the first in her generation of the Churchill clan to sponsor Jedediah.

Jedediah's latest adventure has been in the air, flying with a military officer in his flagship. The trip took them to Scotland, Amsterdam, Newfoundland, London and New York. Jedediah has a log of the trip. Also he has his "short snorter"—a dollar bill signed by all on board, which he earned by making a trip from New York around the world to New York in one continuous flight.

Threadbare, like many other superannuated scholars, he is faint yet pursuing. Here we leave him at the age of seventy years, for later generations of Churchills to try to satisfy his craving for culture and adventure.

8

Dolls in the Victoria and Albert Museum

THE last official public act of Queen Victoria was the laying of the cornerstone of certain new buildings for the South Kensington Museum in London, May 17, 1899. On that occasion she ordered that the name of the museum should be changed to the Victoria and Albert Museum.

Edward VII opened the buildings on June 20, 1909. In that year the Victoria and Albert Museum became purely an art museum for the first time; the scientific collections being opened separately as the "Scientific Museum."

It was in 1825 that Parliament appointed a select committee on arts and manufactures to "inquire into the best means of extending a knowledge of the arts and of the principles of design among the people (especially the manufacturing population of the country)." One of the committee's recommendations was that the opening of public galleries for the people should be encouraged as much as possible.

Not much progress was made in the matter until after the Crystal Palace Exposition in Hyde Park in 1851 had stimulated interest in applied art. In 1852, several collections were purchased from the "Great Exposition" and a museum was opened in the first floor of Marlborough House.

In 1857, the collections at Marlborough House and various other collections, were brought together in South Kensington as "The South Kensington Museum." The first galleries were opened by Queen Victoria on June 2, 1857.

Not the least interesting in the collection are three dolls of the 1774-1780 period, fully dressed and coiffed. The brocades of their dresses are beautiful and their hairdress is both fearful and wonderful.

There are two or more pedlar dolls of the early nineteenth century, at least one of which has a wax face, and there are a number of other wax dolls in the collection.

Doll houses, both English and German, dating back to the seventeenth and eighteenth centuries are in the collection. One that is of particular interest is an early English doll house illustrating the types of domestic utensils used during the age of Queen Anne. Also of interest is a collection of dolls and doll furniture of the eighteenth and nineteenth centuries.

There are several Italian marionette theatres with curtains, footlights and puppets in costume, and miniature furniture, mostly dating to the early half of the eighteenth century.

1

1. Detail of coiffure (1775-1780). Front view

2. Detail of coiffure (1775-1780). Back view

3. English dolls of 1775-1780, fully dressed and coiffed

4. English doll, period of Queen Anne

5. Doll with painted wood body. Topknot headdress of a type introduced from France, beauty patches and silver earrings. About 1690.

All are from Victoria and Albert Museum, London

2

4   5

Left, Doll with head and body of painted wood. Two feet, two and one half inches high with jointed limbs. Early 18th century.

Right, English doll, seventeen and one half inches, wax face representing an elderly woman. About 1800.

Below, English doll dressed to represent lady in court costume. Height nineteen and three quarters inches.

All are from Victoria and Albert Museum, London

Dolls in the Museum of the City of New York

IN 1873 a doting grandmother of old New York wished to give her grandchild a doll with a wardrobe in the very latest fashion and so she sent a dressmaker to Arnold Constable's store to study the latest adult fashions and reproduce them in miniature. This was just the reverse of the usual practice of importing from Paris dolls whose elaborate trousseaux were often copied in adult cloths. A doll similar to the one described is herewith pictured standing beside the Saratoga trunk which contains her wardrobe. Careful inspection will show the elaborate miniature jewelry she wears. This doll is now in the fine collection of early dolls and toys in the Museum of the City of New York, of which Miss Janet Pinney is curator.

The items in the doll and toy collections are largely gifts from the descendants of old New York families and from some modern collectors, and they paint a picture of social life in New York by showing the toys that delighted the New York children of past generations.

Mrs. DeWitt Clinton Cohen, for instance, has donated an interesting collection of jumping jacks.

Miss Pinney has arranged these old playthings attractively in the replica of an old New York toy store, the exhibits being changed from time to time. For boys there are marbles, fire-fighting apparatus, busses, cabs, velocipedes and similar objects. For girls there are stoves, kitchens,

Doll with trunk, about 1875
Museum of the City of New York, New York, N. Y.

cooking dishes, china services, doll carriages, miniature sets of furniture, and for both a collection of early children's books.

Like the Victoria and Albert Museum in London, the Museum of the City of New York has some fine doll houses in its toy collection.

Most interesting for the purposes of this book, however, are the dolls. One of the oldest is an eighteenth century carved and painted doll similar to the ones in the Victoria and Albert Museum.

Perhaps next in interest to collectors is a wire-eyed wax-headed doll with real hair. This is an example of the first type of "sleeping-eye" doll (which came out between 1820 and 1830), the eyes being moved by pulling a wire at the waist. This preceded the type of sleeping eye moved by weights.

Two dolls by Mlle. Calixto Huret, a famous French doll maker of the 1850's, have most elaborate wardrobes which include steamer rugs, paisley shawls, traveling cases, shoes, underwear, dresses, jewels, for every possible occasion. Their history indicates that these dolls were made in 1867 but probably they were made earlier, since we have no evidence

Old New York Toy Shop with woodwork from a store erected in 1827
Museum of the City of New York, New York, N. Y.

that Mlle. Huret was making dolls as late as 1867. One of the advantages of finding a doll with an authenticated history is that it may extend our all too sparse knowledge of early doll makers and their periods of workmanship.

The collection also contains a considerable number of paper dolls of which one of the more interesting is a "Jenny Lind" doll with complete costumes.

A bisque-headed doll with kid body was brought to little Edith Bell in 1843 and subsequently returned with her little mother for a tour of Europe during which she attended an audience with the Pope, probably a unique experience. The doll—using her small mistress as amanuensis—kept a diary of her trip. The diary is now with her in the Museum of the City of New York.

There is a doll trunk in the collection which deserves special mention for it bears the shipping labels that show it to have been shipped with adult trunks. This is probably the only time a small doll trunk has been so shipped.

Left, "Needles and Pins" pedlar doll of about 1860

Right, Doll of about 1850
Both are from Museum of the City of New York, New York, N. Y.

Three dolls, a bisque and two china-headed, are associated with the Civil War period in that they were dressed to be sold at the Sanitary Fair in Brooklyn. The two china-headed dolls are dressed as bride and groom as shown in Chapter 7.

Another French doll with her exquisite wardrobe, complete even to an ermine cape, seal-skin hat and muff and Saratoga trunk, was given to the Museum by Miss Ettie Stettheimer. She received the doll from Dr. Josephine Waller, of Philadelphia, who had won her at the great Centennial Exposition in 1876, commemorating the first hundred years of the Declaration of Independence.

These are but a few of the dolls in the ever-growing toy and doll department of the Museum of the City of New York. How fortunate it is that in this and other museums are being preserved the relics of American childhood that can serve to teach us and future historians so much about the social history of our country.

10

Wooden Dolls

WOODEN dolls are among the earliest that have come down to us from both England and Germany. The Germans worked over a much longer period and were more skilled woodcarvers than the English—a fact evidenced by a comparison of their dolls.

In the author's collection is an English-made wooden doll dating from about 1786. The head and torso are in one piece, turned on a lathe. The body is painted red. Mrs. Imogene Anderson of New York City, who is a collector and expert on early dolls, says that this is only the second one she has ever seen with the body so painted. There are no joints at knees and elbows and the shoulders and hips have the joints simply made with pieces of heavy kid tacked on with handmade nails. The legs and one arm are original and show a most beautiful patina which comes only with age. The right arm is obviously a replacement and does not have the patina. When the doll came to us from a California collection she was dressed in an Empire gown of colored print— an anachronism that jarred our sensibilities so much that we immediately stripped off her clothes and have left her in the "altogether."

A twenty-four-inch wooden doll, evidently German and hand carved, is in the collection of Mrs. Jean Halter of Philadelphia. It is marked in handwriting in ink on the back: "Adelaide Fitz Derby in a visiting dress for 1805." Unfortunately, the dress is no longer with the doll but the inscription dates her.

The same is true of a wooden doll with china head, forearms and lower legs, which has been something of a mystery to the several collectors who have had her. She apparently dates to about 1860 by virtue of her appearance in *Peterson's Magazine* of that decade. She is now in the collection of Mrs. Edmund Poetter. Note that her right hand assumes a peculiar position—as if it was meant to hold something. What was it for? Mrs. Poetter seems to have solved the problem in part, by discovering in *Peterson's Magazine* a picture of a very similar doll fitted out as a "sewing companion." The description of her is as follows:

THE LITTLE COMPANION
by
Mrs. Anna Weaver

"This pretty Little Companion is thus constructed: A wooden doll with china head and legs; a wooden stand and support; a few odd pieces of merino, calico, etc., with which to dress the doll; two papers of needles, a thimble, a pair of scissors and a ball of cotton.

"Cut a piece of wool round, measuring three and a quarter inches in diameter and make a small hole in the center for the piece of stick that supports the doll. The doll measures eight inches from head to foot. Tack on the body a pleated muslin chemisette with long sleeves and over this fashion the petticoat (which should be made of stiff glazed lining) and the skirt of the dress. The latter consists of scarlet French merino with rows of narrow braid put on with steel beads at intervals. Two square pieces of merino laid in front and buttonholed down form the pockets for the needles. The thimble case is also made of merino edged round with bugles and beads and suspended from the waist by a piece of blue ribbon. Another piece of blue ribbon with a ball of cotton threaded on, tie on the right shoulder. The scissors are slipped through a piece of silk cut in the shape of a slipper with two openings in the toe to hold the scissors securely. The headdress which serves the purpose of a pincushion is made of silk, wadded and edged around with lace. A bow of ribbon is placed in front, and strings tie under the chin. To secure the cushion properly it will be necessary to glue it to the head. Now to fasten the doll up to the wooden support, sew the top of the stick firmly to the doll's body, and then glue the other end in the center of the round piece of wood. This done, you have finished this pretty affair which would be especially suitable for a Christmas or New Year's gift."

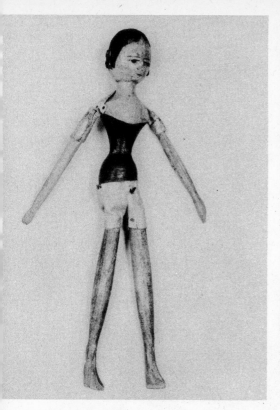

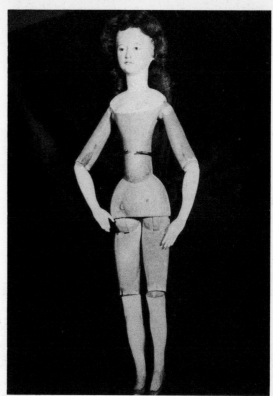

Above left,
All wood doll of about 1786 with joints
    of heavy kid
St. George Collection

Above right,
Wooden doll with hair wig, dating to
    about 1805
Collection of Mrs. Jean Halter,
    Philadelphia, Penna.

Right,
Wooden-bodied doll with china head,
    arms and legs. Foundation of sew-
    ing companion
Collection of Mrs. Edmund Poetter,
    Reading, Vermont

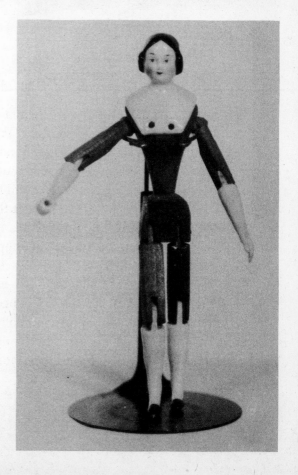

Illustration from *Peterson's Magazine* of the 1860's: Little Sewing Companion
made from wooden-bodied, china-headed doll
Courtesy of Mrs. Edmund Poetter, Reading, Vermont

A German-carved wooden doll head, eight and one-half inches tall, came to us via Westfield, New York. It was brought from Cape Cod a hundred years ago by a family now living in Buffalo, New York. The head bears considerable resemblance to papier-mâché and china heads made in Germany about 1839 and 1840, which is undoubtedly the time this head was made. The inside of the neck has been hollowed out with a chisel and the hair is arranged in a knot at the back of the head.

Mrs. Ralph E. Wakeman supplied her with a body of homespun cotton, linen underwear and a dress of a wool sheer figured in green and orange. We christened her Mary Elizabeth.

Several years ago in a Connecticut antique shop, Mrs. Edmund Poetter found a well-preserved doll with a similar head. It is apparently all original and confirms the tentative date of 1839-1840 for its type. This doll and the one in the author's collection are the only two having

Right,
Old china-headed doll in original clothes
Collection of Mrs. Edmund Poetter,
 Reading, Vermont

Lower right,
"Mary Elizabeth," with rare German-
 carved head
St. George Collection

Lower left,
All original doll, similar to "Mary Eliza-
 beth," with wooden head nailed to
 homespun body
Collection of Mrs. Edmund Poetter,
 Reading, Vermont

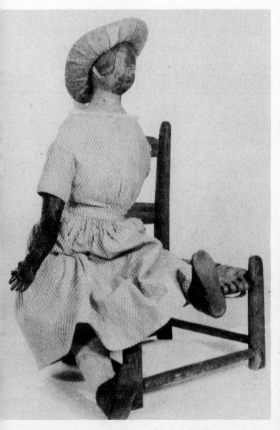

heads of this type, so far as we know, in America. Mrs. Emma C. Clear, who has serviced most of the outstanding doll collections in the country for the last forty years, says she has never seen any like them. The head on the Poetter doll is nailed to the homespun body with handmade nails.

Mr. and Mrs. Grant J. Holt, however, found four similar but smaller heads in a Paris collection and these also are known to be of German origin.

A carved wood head with high hairdo and a comb was given to Mrs. Erwin Chapin of Silver Creek, New York, by a neighbor who said that it had been sent from Germany in 1850 by a doting grandfather to his favorite grandchild. It is quite similar to a doll which the Holts found in the famous Flea Market in Paris. This unusual head is mounted on a body made by Mrs. Clear.

Marie of Burgundy, a doll that was made for Hapsburg royalty, came from Germany to Mrs. Lyle Schmid of Milwaukee, Wisconsin. The real Princess Marie of Burgundy was an ancestress of the Hapsburgs. The doll has head, hands and feet of carved wood painted in oil colors. Her lower legs and train are carved of natural wood. The doll is thirty-two inches tall. She wears the Burgundy cap with two horns and is sumptuously dressed in purple velvet and salmon satin embroidered in gold and colors. Marie is a beautiful creature, fit indeed to be the plaything of some little royal princess.

In the collection of Mrs. Claire Ellegood Smith is a doll with a seventeenth-century carved wood head and shoulders with a high hairdress. She is carved out of a block of solid wood and wears her original clothes.

In the same collection, which contains many rare dolls, is a pair of carved wood children made by the son of Anton Lang, the famous Christus in the Oberammergau Passion Play. The Oberammergau peasantry have long been noted for their skilled woodcarving.

An unusual all-wood, hand-carved crèche doll is in the collection of Miss Helen McEwan of Springfield, Massachusetts. The body of the doll is painted black except for the hands. The head, shown here, is carved with great detail which makes it particularly expressive and beautiful.

In the Bella Landauer collection of advertisements in the New York

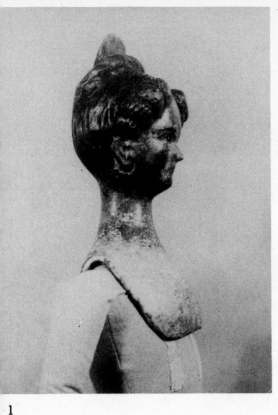

1. Doll with carved-wood head, sent
   from Germany about 1850
Collection of Mrs. Erwin Chapin,
   Silver Creek, New York

2. Detail of the head of the carved-wood
   doll found in the Flea Market, Paris
Collection of Mr. and Mrs. Grant J. Holt,
   Keene, New Hampshire

3. Twenty-seven-and-one-half-inch carved
   wood doll from the Flea Market
Collection of Mr. and Mrs. Grant J. Holt,
   Keene, New Hampshire

1

2

3

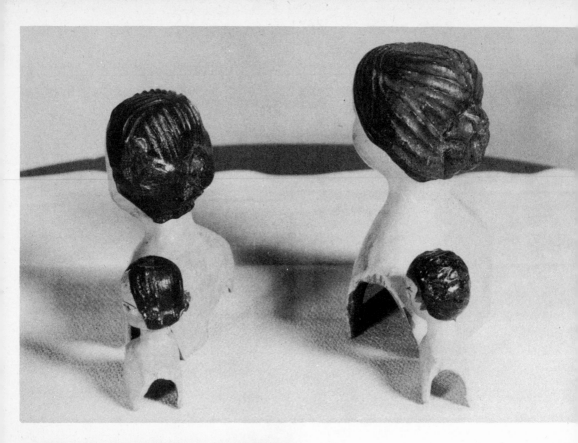

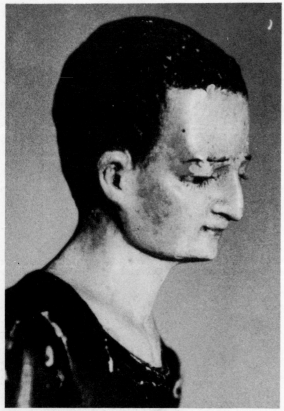

Above,
Four hand-carved wooden heads, similar in workmanship to "Mary Elizabeth" and found in a Paris collection
Collection of Mr. and Mrs. Grant J. Holt, Keene, New Hampshire

Left,
All wood, hand-carved crèche doll
Collection of Miss Helen McEwan, Springfield, Massachusetts

Facing right,
Children carved by the son of Anton Lang, the Christus in the Oberammergau Passion Play in Germany
Collection of Mrs. Claire Ellegood Smith, Hancock, New Hampshire

Facing left,
Doll with German carved-wood head
Collection of Mrs. Claire Ellegood Smith, Hancock, New Hampshire

Historical Museum was found an 1884 advertisement for the Mason and Taylor Springfield, Vermont doll with the patented Johnson turning head.* The Jointed Doll Company was apparently a jobbing firm and is not remembered by any of the older Springfield residents.

Last, but not least in interest, is a tiny colonial wooden peg doll in the collection of Mrs. Ruth Price. She is only two and one-quarter inches tall and wears a thread lace dress which comes from New Bedford, Massachusetts.

* For fuller description of Mason and Taylor doll and Johnson head, see Chapter III of the author's *The Dolls of Yesterday*.

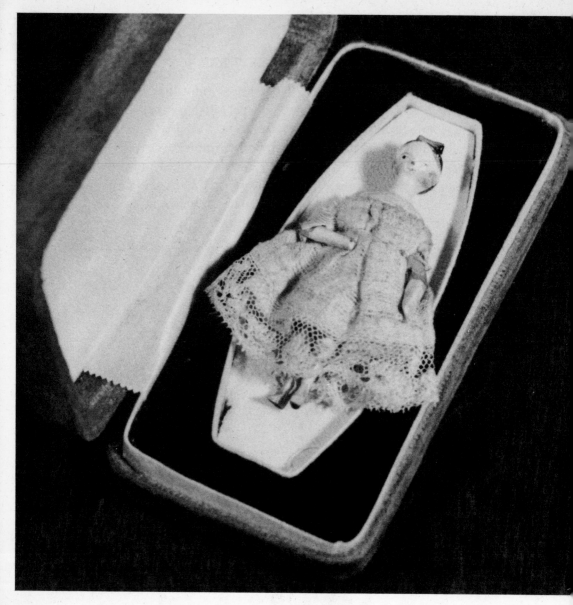

Tiny all wood doll in lace dress
Collection of Mrs. Ruth Price, La Mesa, California

On facing page, top right,
"Marie of Burgundy"—carved and painted wooden doll, made for a Hapsburg
    princess
Collection of Mrs. Lyle Schmid, Milwaukee, Wisconsin

On facing page, below left,
Advertisement of about 1884 for the Mason and Taylor wooden doll made at
                Springfield, Vermont
Courtesy of Mrs. Bella C. Landauer, The Bella C. Landauer Collection, New York
            Historical Museum, New York, New York

Fabric Dolls

FABRIC dolls, whether old or new, have an undeniable charm all their own. The chatelaine of the Victorian doll house in the collection of the Warren County Museum, Lebanon, Ohio, is an example. Home-made, she still has all the charm and individuality of a French fashion doll. In the same collection is another cloth doll that is very appealing. Both probably date back to the Civil War period. *(Shown on page 107.)*

One of the early manufacturers of cloth dolls was Mrs. Izannah Walker of Central Falls, Rhode Island. A few of Mrs. Walker's dolls, made in the 1870's, still survive, but her chief claim to remembrance lies in the fact that the childhood possession of one of her dolls led Mrs. Martha Jenks Chase to make the famous Chase dolls. Through the kindness of Mrs. Ruth Price of La Mesa, California, an old friend and former neighbor of the Chase family at Pawtucket, Rhode Island, we were brought into contact with Mrs. Ruth Chase Howland of New York, one of the three daughters of Martha Chase. Mrs. Howland's letter is given in part:

"I will send this sketch of some of the facts about the dolls and the characteristics of Martha Chase, or 'Mattie' as we and our friends used to call her after we grew up. It was indicative of her young spirit and companionable nature that it seemed natural to give her the loving nick-name.

"Born in 1851, she was the daughter of Dr. James L. Wheaton, a well-to-do physician who was well known in Rhode Island in those days.

At that time it was customary for young medical students to get part of their training and experience in the offices of practicing physicians. Among those who studied with Dr. Wheaton was Julian A. Chase, whom Martha Wheaton married. They had seven children, two of whom died in infancy. In bringing up her children Martha Chase developed an unusual insight and understanding of child psychology, as if she herself still retained the unspoiled and pure spirit of a child.

"She was very ingenious in making all sorts of toys and favors for the various parties she planned for the happiness of her children, and it was perhaps an inevitable development that she made dolls. Our home was the congregating center for all the children in the neighborhood, and they too shared in the good times she planned for us. As a little girl, 'Mattie' owned one of the Walker dolls, which later was much admired by her own children. By that time Mrs. Walker had passed on and the patent for her dolls had expired. With that doll in mind Mrs. Chase experimented and invented a method for making a similar doll for her children. Soon all of the children of her friends wanted dolls so she made them for those children.

"It was after one of her own daughters wanted to take a doll to a little friend in Calais, Maine, and Mrs. Chase took the doll to Boston to the Jordan Marsh store to have shoes fitted to it, that she began to make the dolls commercially. That was about 1897. The buyer of the doll department happened to see her fitting the shoes to her doll, and asked her where she got it. When she said she made it herself, he wanted to give her an order at once. But she told him she had no thought of making dolls to sell. After some urging, she finally agreed to discuss the matter at home, and if decided in the affirmative, she would send him a trial order of a dozen dolls. From that incident her business grew rapidly, and dolls traveled to all parts of this country, and into far distant countries.

"The doll, as originally designed by Mrs. Chase, was made of stockinet and cotton cloth, stuffed with cotton batting. It had molded hard raised features, with painted face and hair. Only the arms, legs, and head were painted, the torso being covered with sateen. Later a stockinet cover for the torso was substituted, waterproofed and painted so that the doll could be bathed.

"Besides the regular doll she made many character dolls; several Dickens characters, George Washington, a colored mammy, some of the characters in *Alice in Wonderland*, and a few tiny dolls—exact counterparts of the larger doll but only about six or seven inches long. (*Shown on page 109.*) Most of these dolls are no longer made—therefore those in existence are sought by collectors.

"Always interested in sewing, she not only taught her own three daughters to sew, but also held sewing classes in the Sunday school rooms of her church every week. A little later she convinced the Superintendent of Public Schools of the desirability of domestic science education in the city schools. For a year she conducted the classes in a near-by school house, paying for all supplies herself and bearing all other expenses. She was instrumental also in the forming of the Girls' Club of the Lorraine Manufacturing Company and for several years led the club.

"For many years Martha Chase confined her manufacturing to toy dolls, until, in about the year 1910, she received a request from a hospital in Hartford, Connecticut, for a life size doll for the training of nurses. And from that beginning there has grown a business which supplies life-size mannikins which are sent to hospitals all over the world.

"Mrs. Chase was active in her business up to the day of her death in August, 1925, leaving to us who knew her a happy memory of her loyalty, optimism, kindness, ingenuity, humor, youthful spirit, and innate goodness.

"In your letter to Mrs. Price you asked for information about 'Mrs. Walker' and data concerning her dolls. I think that perhaps Mrs. Price had reference to the same Walker who made the doll my mother had as a child. Her name was Izannah F. Walker, and she lived in Central Falls, Rhode Island, which is not more than a couple of miles from where my mother was born in Pawtucket. I don't know her date of birth, but know that she was of the generation just before my mother's.

"The Chase dolls are still being made in improved designs and the business is being managed by one of Mrs. Chase's grandsons. Most of the business is the manufacturing of the large hospital dolls."

In Europe, notable fabric dolls were made by Madame Lenci in Italy and Frau Kathe Kruse in Germany. The Lenci dolls were made of pieces of felt pressed together under pressure and their hollow limbs and bodies were almost as hard as wood. There were many types ranging from clown dolls the size of clothespins to beautiful boudoir dolls representing Raquel Miller, the dancer. The most charming of all were her child dolls.

Victorian doll house
Collection of the Warren County
Museum, Lebanon, Ohio

Old rag doll
Collection of the Warren County
Museum, Lebanon, Ohio

 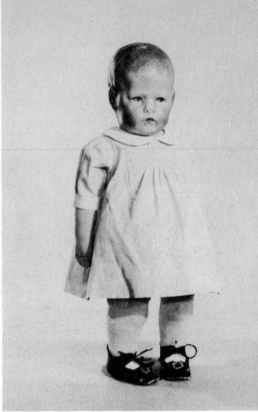

Left, Two Lenci dolls   *Right,* Kathe Kruse doll
Both are from St. George Collection

Their clothing was usually of felt or felt combined with chiffon. All Madame Lenci's dolls were marked with exquisite taste, for Madame Lenci was an artist before she became a doll maker. Madame Lenci is now dead but her factory which was closed during the war—World War II—has been re-opened.

Frau Kathe Kruse was an invalid in pre-war Germany who started making dolls representing charming German toddlers. She first made them for her own children. Then, like Martha Chase, she went into business, built a factory, and world-wide trade was the result. During the war, Frau Kruse fell under the displeasure of Adolph Hitler because her dolls reflected in their faces the maker's own sorrow over the state of her country and the death in battle of her own young son. Hitler closed the factory and forbade the artist to make more dolls. Frau Kruse outlived the war and has re-opened her doll factory.

Many Indian dolls may be classed as fabric dolls. Like the famous Eugene Field collection, described and pictured in the author's *The Dolls*

A group of Chase dolls exhibited at the National Doll Show
Collection of Mrs. Ruth Price, La Mesa, California

of Yesterday, Indian dolls are usually made of leather or kidskin trimmed with beads. Pictured here are two Indian dolls from the collection of Mrs. Philip Cummings of Woodstock, Vermont. One is a Sioux Indian doll, about fifty years old, of gray kidskin elaborately trimmed with turquoise blue beads. The other doll of more recent origin is a Navajo with hand-hammered ornaments. It represents a weaver at her loom.

The Ravca dolls originated in France before the war but are now being made in the United States. Bernard M. Ravca and Frances Eleanor Ravca, his wife, are "folks" in the sense in which that term is used in our southern states; gentle, clever and intelligent, they are real artists as well. Many have been making portrait dolls and character dolls since Bernard Ravca began his career some twenty-five years ago, but none has quite equalled the artistic quality of his work. One need not seek far for the reason, of course, for he is a born artist, and artists are born, not made. This artistic gift, in Mr. Ravca's case, is supplemented by wide travel and by keen observation, not only of racial costumes and habits, but individual faces as well. Mr. Ravca, being an artist, does not go in for mass production and, as he himself will tell you, his entire annual production is only about ninety dolls.

Bernard M. Ravca was born in Paris in 1904. His early ambition was to study medicine, but, lacking funds for the long, expensive education, after his father's death, he went to work in a studio just outside Paris, painting scarves, shawls and doll faces.

He conceived the idea that dolls should be as individual as people are. His first success was a doll representing Marguerite in *Faust*. His second, a pair of French character types for an English lord to present to his wife as a silver wedding gift, attracted so much attention that he was able to open his own studio and take up the work of doll making in real earnest. In the years that followed, his dolls have become world-famous and he has won some thirty medals and awards in competition with doll makers of forty-two nations.

In 1938, when the King and Queen of England were the guests of President LeBrun of France, one of the five rooms of the royal suite was decorated with his French provincial dolls. In 1939, the French government sent Mr. Ravca and his dolls to take part in the New York Exposition at Flushing Meadows as part of the French exhibits.

Before the World's Fair was ended, France had been over-run by the

Above, Navajo Indian weaver. Rag doll
   with jewelry of pure silver
Collection of Mrs. Philip Cummings,
   Woodstock, Vermont

Sioux Indian doll about fifty years old.
   Note turquoise beadwork on shoul-
   ders and moccasins
Collection of Mrs. Philip Cummings,
   Woodstock, Vermont

Germans. His studio was looted and his family gone. Remaining in the United States, he devoted the proceeds of his lectures to work with French orphans and to relief organization. He displayed and sold his dolls, as he does now, in large department stores in the principal cities.

The collection that he brought to the World's Fair naturally consisted of French provincial types, but he has since expanded the collection to include types from many countries throughout the world. Since he has married an American girl and taken out American citizenship, Mr. Ravca is devoting much of his attention to the varied American types and to American historical dolls.

The faces of most of his dolls are made of silk stockings, but he also makes use of an unusual material, chemically treated bread crumbs. These are used largely in miniatures and closely resemble wax.

One of the first of his bread-crumb group sold in America is in the fine collection of Mrs. Grace Perlberg of New York, where the material has stood the test of time and answers the question as to whether such materials are durable.

Mr. Ravca says, however, that he can only make these faces successfully from the French bread of France, since it contains some ingredient —possibly gluten—that is absent in such large quantities in the flour from which the French bread of the United States is made. Mr. Ravca's bread-crumb dolls are remarkable for the detail and accuracy of their costumes.

A pair that Mr. Ravca, himself, considers to be among the finest dolls he has ever made is the organ grinder, which plays "La Marseillaise," pictured with the musical dolls in Chapter 1, and the pedlar doll pictured in Chapter 16. These two dolls are really a pair, husband and wife. They were first shown at Mr. Ravca's exhibit at Lord & Taylor.

Another musical group—one that is silent, however—is the "Concert," which shows an orchestra with various instruments accompanying a prima donna at the extreme right of the group.

Mrs. Frances Ravca, the former Frances Eleanor Dieks of Cohoes, N. Y., has been a doll maker in her own right since she was a girl of sixteen in high school. One of her early dolls, Helen Hayes as *Victoria Regina*, is owned by Mrs. Norman Craven of Detroit and Quechee, Vermont, and two others, characters from *Little Women*, are in the collection of Mrs. Lee Anderson of Woodstock, Vermont. Mrs. Ravca

"Concert"—a group by Bernard M. Ravca
Courtesy of the Ravcas

attended the New York School of Fine and Applied Arts after receiving preliminary art training in Troy and Albany. This training, together with her later marriage to Bernard Ravca, has ripened her art to a fine maturity.

One of her most charming groups might be called "Grandfather Tales." It consists of an old Turkish grandfather sitting cross-legged on the floor, while his twelve-year-old granddaughter sits beside him raptly listening to the Arabian Nights story her grandfather is relating. The family baby sleeps peacefully strapped to her back.

Another group that is realistic consists of an old, old street cleaner, a "White Wings," pausing in his work for a bit of friendly banter with an old lady, market-bound, with her basket on her arm.

Still another group of human interest might be called "Golden Wedding." It is one in which an elderly woman displays their golden wedding cake to her elderly husband.

113

Both Mr. and Mrs. Ravca are endowed with a keen sense of humor which shows in most of their dolls. Many are caricatures such as "The Brat." An American grandmother is holding the new baby of the family on her lap while the child who has been displaced, a little girl looking every inch a "brat," approaches holding out a spray of flowers in her right hand. In the left hand concealed behind her back is a dead rat, typifying the jealous and unhappy thoughts that are in her heart. At the back, left, a cat eyes the dead rat.

The dolls of both the Ravcas are interesting and unique and worthy of a place in the finest collections. They will surely be heirlooms in the future.

Below,
"Golden Wedding"—by Frances Eleanor Ravca
Courtesy of the Ravcas

On facing page,
"Grandfather Tales"—by Frances Eleanor Ravca
Courtesy of the Ravcas

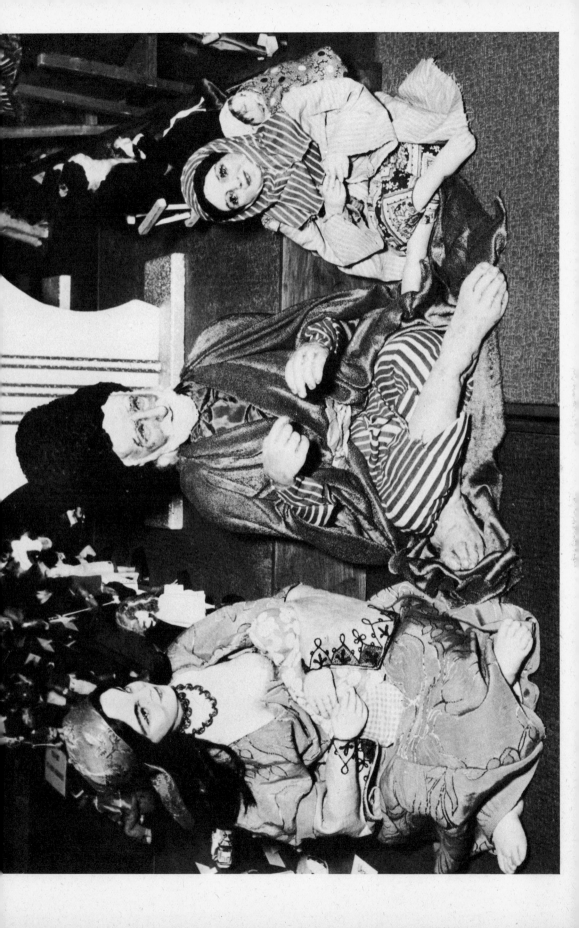

China Dolls

CHINA head dolls exceed all others in numbers and in variety of models, and one is always discovering new kinds. Some seem to have been made by the finest factories and others by small makers in backyard kilns. In fact, they vary so much in the quality of workmanship that there seems little doubt that their manufacture was largely a home industry. China head dolls were made almost exclusively in Germany.

One of the interesting heads that has come to light is the one of the young Mozart, so beautifully displayed at the National Doll Show at the Charles W. Bowers Memorial Museum. The furniture in the room in which he was displayed—appropriately enough, miniature musical furniture—was made by Miss Helen Armitage.

Another rare piece in the same show is the sleeping baby which experts pronounced to be Dresden and which is signed by an individual artist. B. H. Leffingwell of Rochester, New York, offered us a slightly different version of the same baby, the blanket being flowered instead of plaid, but it is undoubtedly a rare museum piece.

Equally beautiful and rare are the queenly beauties that were found in Vienna by Mr. and Mrs. Grant J. Holt of Keene, New Hampshire. The one on the extreme left of the picture is Marie Antoinette, the wife of Louis XVI of France. Her hairdress is exquisite and she wears a court dress of old brocade with an under panel of old silk.

The central figure is Madame Casileri. She is seated in a marvelously carved chair of wood and gold leaf. The figure is exquisitely fine china, probably Dresden. In her hand is a prayer book. (History says she was very religious and often carried her prayer book.) She wears a necklace of ruby and gold beads and the same decoration is around her hat which is of purple china. Under her feet is a blue cushion. Her dress is of old brocade and lace dotted with real green amber set in gold.

The figure on the right is Madame de Pompadour, the mistress of King Louis XIV of France. The head and legs are exquisite china. She has golden slippers. Her dress is of changeable taffeta. She holds her jewel case in her hands, symbolizing her love of jewels.

A rare china doll from the collection of Mrs. Edna Fletcher of Newburgh, New York, has large blown glass eyes of dark brown. Her hair is arranged much like a Greiner and she looks amazingly like a papier-mâché.

A large Jenny Lind which the Holts found in Paris is beautiful. She is dressed in heavy cream-colored corded silk.

Mrs. Arthur Hillsdorf of Syracuse, New York, has among the interesting china dolls in her collection a pink lustre with a hair wig from France. The head is cut out under the wig, showing that it is early, of the period when duty from Germany was charged by the kilowatt and doll heads were cut out at the top to reduce the weight. The head is glazed inside and out. Another doll from the collection is "Lydia Merrick," who has her hair arranged with a braid around her head.

The blonde head of the type called Godey or "Curly Top" is rather rare. Mrs. F. F. Hockaday of the Boston Doll Hospital has a similar head that is still more unusual. The front of the hair is arranged back to the crown in the same manner as the head in the author's collection but then there is a black band and the hair back of that hangs free.

Mrs. Lydia Bowerman began doll collecting as a hobby when she was an office employee of the New York Central Railway in New York. Since her retirement from the business world she has maintained her own private collection and also has helped other collectors after becoming a dealer. She is associated with a well-known antique dealer in Milan, Ohio, exhibits at many of the antique shows and is an active member of the Detroit Unit, No. 21, of the National Doll and Toy Collectors Club. Thus it can be seen that Mrs. Bowerman really knows and understands old dolls, and so the group picture of some china dolls from her personal collection will bear careful study. One of the most noteworthy is the clown doll at the extreme right of the picture.

Many of the dolls in this chapter are one of a kind and therefore beyond the reach of the average collector. Not so the dolls in the Bowerman group, most of which, though rare, are still obtainable occasionally.

Very rare indeed is the "Frozen Charlotte" from the collection of Mrs. Henry Peterson of Austin, Texas. The pose of the doll is unique in Frozen Charlottes, standing as it does with folded arms. It is one and three quarters inches tall and is of pink lustre china.

Three rare china head dolls found in Vienna. *Left to right:* Marie Antoinette, Madame Casileri and Madame de Pompadour
Collection of Mr. and Mrs. Grant J. Holt, Keene, New Hampshire

On facing page,
The young Mozart, in china, with miniature musical furniture made by Miss Helen Armitage
Courtesy Charles W. Bowers Memorial Museum, National Doll Show, 1949, Santa Ana, California

Dresden sleeping baby as displayed at the National Doll Show, 1949
Courtesy Charles W. Bowers Memorial Museum, Santa Ana, California

Right,
Thirty-two inch, china head Jenny Lind
    brought from Paris
Collection of Mr. and Mrs. Grant J. Holt,
    Keene, New Hampshire

Left,
Unusual china doll with large, pupil-less
    blown glass eyes
Collection of Mrs. Edna Fletcher,
    Newburgh, New York

Above,
Group of unusual old china dolls. Note clown doll at extreme right of picture
Collection of Mrs. Lydia Bowerman, Milan, Ohio

Left,
"Lydia Merrick" with a braid around the top of her china head
Collection of Mrs. Arthur Hillsdorf, Syracuse, New York

On facing page,
1. Two china dolls. One on right, made of pink lustre, has head cut out under wig
Collection of Mrs. Arthur Hillsdorf, Syracuse, New York

2. China head known as Godey doll, or "Curly Top"
St. George Collection

3. Pink lustre "Frozen Charlotte" only one and three-quarters inches high
Collection of Mrs. Henry Peterson, Austin, Texas

1

2

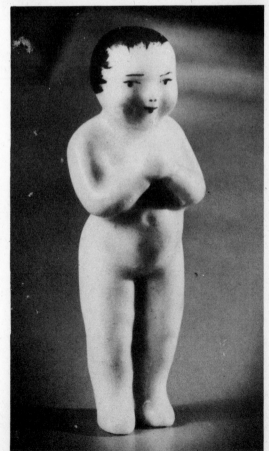

3

Wax Dolls

AFTER being neglected in favor of other types, the wax dolls are finally coming into their own with collectors, and for good reasons. With the possible exception of carved wood dolls, wax dolls are as old as any. In the age of Queen Anne both wooden and wax dolls were made and quite a few of both have come down to us. All through the nineteenth century wax was used as a medium, probably most extensively from 1870 to the late 1890's. Of course the finest wax dolls were made by the Montanaris in England but they were not alone in the creation of this type.

Many of the English and German-made wax heads had a papier-mâché foundation with just a thin coating of wax. The French made thick wax heads similar to the Montanari dolls. Many wax dolls, especially the cheaper variety, were made in Germany.

During the 1870's to the 1880's, when wax dolls were in their heyday, many types of hairdos were used, and often the pompadours, lengthwise or crosswise, were molded on the heads themselves with the hair or mohair crowns over them. These late wax-over-papier-mâché dolls quite often had pierced ears and earrings.

Many wax dolls have perished because of the ravages of heat and cold to which they are so susceptible, or have fallen prey to small brothers and sisters who sometimes used the wax in lieu of chewing gum. However, if one does find a damaged wax doll they are much more easily repaired than bisques and chinas. There are many studios that specialize in renewing the wax, which, let us add, is not a job for the amateur.

In the northwest, Lewis Sorenson, doll maker of Bellingham, Washington, does excellent work; and in the east is Mrs. Ralph E. Wakeman of Claremont, New Hampshire, whose work in waxing dolls has been notable.

One of the most remarkable jobs of wax restoration that has come to our attention was that of the seventeenth century figure of "Moses," belonging to Mrs. William Biggert of California, done by Mrs. Wakeman. Nothing remained of the figure except the head, and even that was completely broken off at the back of the neck. Before beginning work on the figure, Mrs. Wakeman studied carefully the work of Doré and other Biblical illustrators. The head with missing parts restored was mounted with wax hands and feet on a body made of very old linen. The robes were also made of old linen and purple silk. Moses is represented as coming down from Mt. Sinai with the tables of the law.

Before shipping the figure to California, Mrs. Wakeman had it on display for certain guests in an appropriate setting in her home. Jewish rabbi and Catholic priest alike spent much time in reverent contemplation of the figure.

Two other excellent examples of Mrs. Wakeman's rewaxing and costuming of dolls are the pair from the collection of Mrs. John Alexander of South Royalton, Vermont, pictured with Mrs. Alexander's small daughter.

Old wax dolls made in France are usually of the thick wax types, like the Madame Montanari dolls, with hair and eyebrows set in individually.

Such is the exquisite "Child Jesus" found by Mr. and Mrs. Grant Holt, Keene, New Hampshire, in a Paris antique shop. It is twenty-six inches tall with thick wax head, hands and feet. The body is of old linen. The soft curls that cover the head, the eyebrows and eyelashes are set in individually. The robe is crimson velvet trimmed with gold fringe and slipped over the left arm is a crown of thorns. It was evidently a church figure or perhaps was made for a private shrine.

An old twenty-five-inch wax doll, dating to about 1850, is in the collection of Miss Maude E. Willand. Its wax hair is braided and wound around the head and, with a cloth body, it has wooden hands and feet.

Modern Mexico is skilled in the making of wax dolls, especially character dolls. By some secret process, these are supposed to be impervious to extremes of heat and cold, which most wax dolls are not.

A local collector bought a pair of these dolls while visiting in Mexico and brought them home by airplane. When she unpacked her dolls, she found to her dismay that the faces were badly cracked in all directions. "But, yes," said a pilot friend, "that was caused by air pressure. Had you come home by train nothing would have happened to them." So modern transportation adds a new hazard to the life of wax dolls.

Another mishap occurred when a California collector bought a beautiful Montanari doll in the East in the summer of 1949 and took it home in her car. It will be remembered that the summer of 1949 was particularly hot and driving across the desert the wax head of the Montanari softened in its box so that one side of the face dropped down. A visit to a wax modeling studio will be necessary to repair the damage. Had the owner loosened the head from the body and stuffed the head firmly full of crushed tissue paper, the damage would not have occurred. The Montanari and thick French wax heads have no reinforcements of papier-mâché and therefore are more easily damaged by extreme heat. They should not be shipped without being carefully stuffed.

Bisque dolls with teeth came in after 1880 but wax dolls with teeth never were plentiful. Miss Marion Smith has a beautiful wax doll with three teeth. Mrs. Erwin Chapin of Silver Creek, New York, has in her collection an old wax doll with some wooden peg teeth driven in. Mrs. Chapin also has another old wax doll in original condition that measures seven inches in height.

The Warren County Museum in Lebanon, Ohio, has an interesting wax doll in its collection with a molded hairdo in the waterfall style that prevailed between 1850 and 1860, which helps to date the doll.

In the writer's collection are two wax dolls of the 1870 period with pompadours molded on the heads. One doll has on her original tan silk dress of the period. Her head has been rewaxed by Mrs. Wakeman and her tightly curled wig, also made by Mrs. Wakeman, is an exact copy of the original. The one on the right has a pompadour molded on her head over which a mohair wig is combed and covered with a net. This latter is a rather unusual type of the cheaper wax dolls. The ears are pierced for earrings.

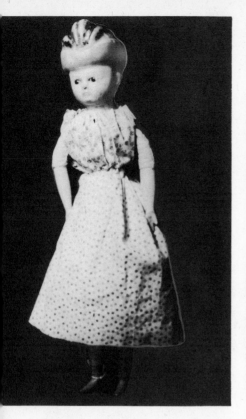 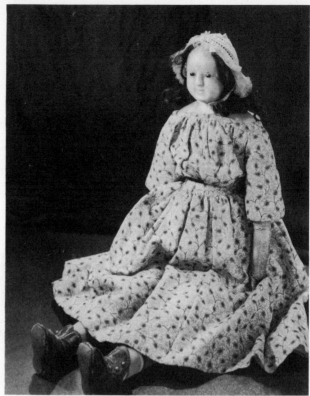

Left, Wax doll with three-feathered hat molded on its head
Courtesy B. H. Leffingwell, Rochester, New York

Right, Twenty-six-inch wax doll of about 1820. Unusual in this size
St. George Collection

It can be seen that wax dolls come in great variety and are intriguing enough to warrant a collector's specializing in them alone. Moreover, they are, for the most part, less expensive than dolls of other types.

As intriguing as any wax dolls we have seen are two in the collection of Mrs. Jean Halter of Philadelphia. The doll on the right (*Page 137*) is eighteenth century, probably about a hundred and fifty years old. She seems to be all original. Her clothes are of that period. Her head is solid lump wax, her arms and legs the original cloth. Her hair is set in.

The doll on the left is about 1845 and is also all original. She has blue leather arms and her hair is set in. Her dress is pink taffeta.

WAX DOLLS FROM THE CANAL ZONE

It seems indeed strange that so colorful a country as either Panama or Central America should have produced no native folk dolls, but that is the fact that Kansas-born Mrs. K. P. MacDowell discovered accom-

127

Seventeenth century "Moses" restored by Mrs. Ralph E. Wakeman
Collection of Mrs. William Biggert, Los Angeles, California

Louise Alexander receiving a visit from two wax lady dolls restored and costumed
by Mrs. Ralph E. Wakeman
Collection of Mrs. John Alexander, South Royalton, Vermont

panying her husband to Panama when he went there on a limited assignment for the United States government. Her husband's work made
it necessary to fly over a good deal of territory, trips on which Mrs.
MacDowell frequently accompanied him, so that she has had most
interesting experiences.

Mrs. MacDowell calls herself a "doll-lover rather than a doll-
collector" so naturally, she looked for dolls on her travels and was amazed
to find that there were no dolls.

Being a resourceful woman, Mrs. MacDowell set about experimenting with various mediums to supply the need. We cannot do better
than to let Mrs. MacDowell tell her own story, as she wrote it in answer
to the author's inquiry:

"To most of us Panama is the little narrow isthmus where the United
States maintains the Panama Canal. It is tiny to be sure, where the
'fastest' railroad in the world travels from the Atlantic to the Pacific in
one hour. Five minutes or little more in the air and you can see the
Pacific; then turn your head and there is the blue Atlantic. Yet tiny as

129

Indian woman and baby
Doll made by Mrs. K. P. MacDowell, Pedro Miguel, Canal Zone

Facing page,
Above, Indian girl in festival dress
Doll made by Mrs. K. P. MacDowell, Pedro Miguel, Canal Zone

Below, Indian children
Wax dolls made by Mrs. K. P. MacDowell, Pedro Miguel, Canal Zone

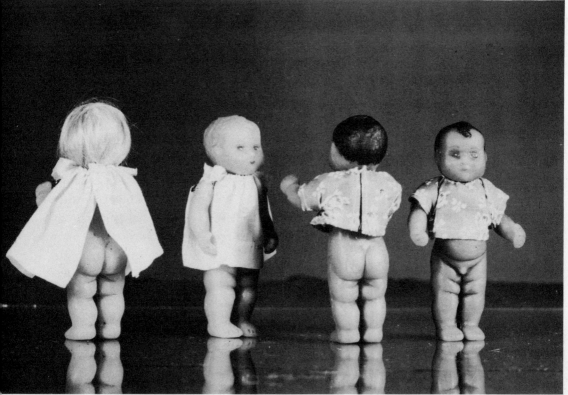

it is there is a world of interest for those who care to venture out of the Canal Zone.

"There are very dense jungles inhabited by several species of monkeys, pumas, ocelot, jaguar; and black panthers have been known to prowl around even the more densely populated towns.

"The people of the wealthier class are Spanish but the majority of people are Indian, colored and mixed.

"In the larger towns the people dress as we do but during carnival the costumes are a riot of color. The 'polleras' worn by the girls are heirlooms made of very fine linen very intricately cross stitched and trimmed with handmade lace. At least a year is spent in the making of these costumes and the value of a dress alone is around $150. The jewelry worn with the 'pollera' is of pure gold consisting of a long flat chain of which each link represents a fish scale and ends with a flexible fish of gold. The skirts are fastened with two gold buttons on each side. On the left shoulder is worn by those fortunate enough to own one, an ornament of gold dug out of one of the ancient Indian graves near the Costa Rican border.

"The hair is always parted in the center with a 'biscuit' wound low on each side of the neck. Gold combs are worn on either side of the part and many ornaments fashioned of gold wire and beads fastened to hair pins are scattered in pairs through the hair. Sometimes red carnations are worn in place of the beads. The slippers are heelless and must match in color the yarn pompons and ribbons worn both at the back and front of the dress.

"The girls who cannot afford the elaborate dress wear the 'pollera montuna' which consists of the pollera blouse with a calico skirt made in two wide ruffles edged with a narrow one. She wears her hair in two long braids and a straw hat.

"The man in his 'montuno' is quite a sight. The shirt is half way to the knee and edged with fringe. They are very elaborately cross stitched in bright colors. The trousers end half way below the knee and are usually fringed too. Since the suit has no pockets, he carries a bag (which has probably been crocheted by his wife) hanging from his shoulder. It is said the amount of handwork put into these suits and bags shows the affection the wife has for her husband. His shoes are very simple flat sandals probably made by himself and tied with what material is available. The hat is of Panamanian fiber and has a bit of black woven in. Usually the front is fastened to the crown with a bright yarn pompon and a ribbon of the same color falls down the back in streamers.

"The montuno and montuno pollera are habitually worn by some of the people in the remote villages. Many of these people proudly display a set of teeth filed to points.

"The Indian women of the San Blas Islands are unique. They never leave the island and a trip to visit them is quite an undertaking. The islands are an archipelago lying off the northeast coast of the Isthmus extending to near the Colombian border. This sounds very near, yet it is a rugged, very rugged, several days journey in a small boat or an hour by air over the Darien province, noted for its hostile head hunting Indians. The landing strip, being very short on the mainland near the island we visited, made it necessary to go in a three passenger Piper Cub. A bit risky, but after reaching home safely you decide it was worth every bit of the risk. I have waited three years for this trip and the opportunity to see the real Indians in their colorful costumes.

"Our mode of travel from the landing strip to the island was a cayuca which is a canoe-like boat hollowed out of a huge mahogany log. A few minutes and we were near enough to see the group of women standing on the beach with their brilliant blouses and head dresses. A bit nearer and we could see the gold nose rings and the huge gold ear ornaments. Several little albino children were among the group. We were told these children are the result of inter-marriage in the effort to keep their race pure.

"The blouses worn by the women and little girls are the most unique bits of handwork I have ever seen. Designs usually of birds or animals with a bit of lettering are appliquéd in layers—each edge being turned under so neatly that the stitches are not visible. A sarong, predominantly blue, is wrapped around the waist and tucked in at the side to hold it on. Shoes are never worn but the ankles are wrapped with strings of beads tightly wound to keep the legs small. The wrists are also wrapped in the same manner. The scarf worn on the head is always red with yellow print.

"The little boys wear quite a costume, simply a wreath of red flowers gathered in the jungles on the mainland and tied around the head and perhaps one or several necklaces of animal or fish teeth.

"These costumes are never seen by the tourist unless he happens to be there during the carnival which takes place three days before Lent. The one costume, though, that is seen by every tourist is the little every-day Panamanian in his camiseta which is just a short shirt and nothing more. It seems that the law says he must wear one garment and for some reason the shirt is chosen. You don't forget the little bare bottoms seen in Colón and Panama City. Yet when they do dress up you should see the boys' fancy little satin suits trimmed with lace!

"For ten years Mr. MacDowell has been in and out of Central and South America and when asked to bring some Panamanian dolls the answer always was 'There are no dolls in Panama.' I discovered it to be true when we came here for our limited assignment.

"To make them myself was the only answer and you would be greatly surprised to know how long it has taken to learn in detail just what should go into each costume. A friend, Mrs. John Yarbrough, who now is in Washington, D. C., finally came through with all the needed information and we started making the dolls of wire and rayon, covering the faces with georgette dyed a suitable shade. We were never quite pleased with them but enjoyed working with them. Her time was up a year ago and when she returned I began to look for some other way of making the dolls.

"We really started something, for while I was working with this and that, trying to find the right thing, the stores blossomed out with many dolls in polleras and montunas as well as models of the San Blas Indians. They were just the hard-bodied, inexpensive composition eight-inch dolls and nothing that I would want—especially the Indians with shoes and socks molded on their feet.

"At first I tried rubber molds, thinking of pouring plaster in them, but that was not the answer. Then bisque seemed to be right when I learned there was a ceramic class being held in Balboa. After investigating that— it, too, seemed hopeless, as I would surely want my own oven and to have one shipped down here for our short stay was too expensive.

"Mr. MacDowell had kept a pan of beeswax he used several months ago to coat a wire coil he wound for a radio part. Running onto that started me thinking: why not try that? Stacks of books were brought home from the library trying to learn something about the coloring and painting of wax but there wasn't a bit of useful information—so I had to work it out for myself as best I could.

"To start with, plaster for molds is quite a problem in this damp tropical climate. The wax stuck and if I greased the mold the paint wouldn't dry. After several tries an Indian that was good enough to dress finally came out. I sent that one to "Mama" Clear not because I was proud of the doll at all but because I did like the idea and the effect. Her encouragement and suggestions resulted in the little camiseta baby I have always wanted to make and then, with things going so much more smoothly, the pollera girl was tried. These are all first attempts and now I want to model them in more detail.

"The first thing I ever tried to model was a sleeping baby head and hands. 'Mama' Clear said they would fire it for me but the clay was unsuitable so I did nothing more with it until recently. I made a solid wax head and hands and tried to set the hair in the wax. I needed a baby for a fifty-year-old baby doll outfit that was on an old jointed doll. It is a bit rough but from a short distance looks quite relaxed and sound asleep."

It was Mrs. Clear who called our attention first to the outstanding work that Mrs. MacDowell is doing, not only as an artist in wax doll making but in her thorough research into the costumes and customs of these interesting Indians. She feels, as we do, that Mrs. MacDowell is making a distinct contribution to the doll hobby as well as to the folk culture of our country. She believes that Mrs. MacDowell's doll will one day rank with those of such wax doll makers as Mme. Augusta Montanari and Grace Storey Putnam.

Mrs. Clear also feels, as we do, that lovely as ceramic dolls are, there is a wide field for wax dolls. Collectors have been neglecting this field which, when explored, will amaze them with its possibilities. The photographs on the next pages illustrate many of the charms of these wax dolls.

Above, Child Jesus, found in Paris antique shop
Collection of Mr. and Mrs. Grant J. Holt, Keene, New Hampshire

Wax doll remarkable for the fact that hair combines the Montanari method with a partial wig
Collection of Mrs. Alice Williams, Mechanics' Falls, Maine

Wax doll resembling Queen Victoria
Collection of Miss Marian L. Smith,
    Burlington, Vermont

Below,
Two unusual and beautiful early wax
    dolls
Collection of Mrs. Jean Halter,
    Philadelphia, Penna.

Twenty-five-inch wax doll of about 1850 with intricate wax hairdo
Collection of Miss Maude E. Willand, Manchester, New Hampshire

Wax doll of about 1860 with waterfall
hairdo
Courtesy Warren County Museum,
Lebanon, Ohio

All original, seven-inch old wax doll
Collection of Mrs. Erwin Chapin,
Silver Creek, New York

Wax doll with teeth
Collection of Miss Marian L. Smith,
Burlington, Vermont

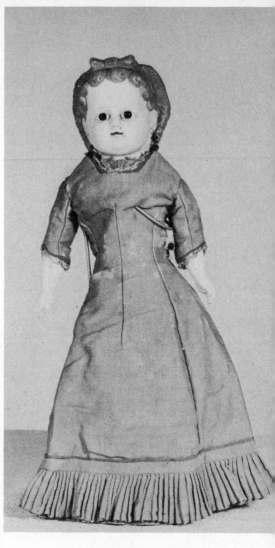

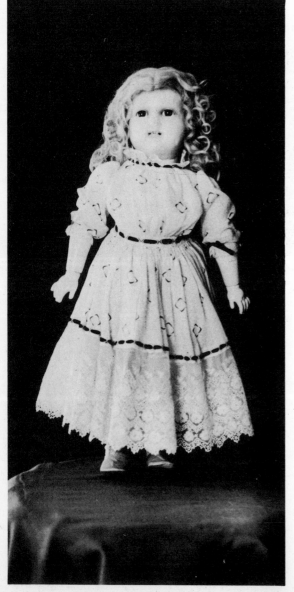

Old wax doll with several wooden teeth
Collection of Mrs. Erwin Chapin,
Silver Creek, New York

Papier-Mâché Dolls

IN the term "milliners' model," milliner is not used in the modern sense of "hat maker" but rather in the older sense of the term—supplier of women's clothing. Therefore, these little papier-mâché dolls with stiff, jointless, kid bodies and crude wooden arms and legs are oftentimes referred to as "dressmaker dolls." They are also hairdressers' models as can readily be seen by the wide variation in their coiffures.

Although papier-mâché was in use for other purposes, it appears to have been used first for doll heads about 1820. Apparently these models were made up to about 1860. It is quite easy to judge the age of the little dolls by the style of hairdress.

Curiously enough, who made these early little dolls and where they were made is still one of the unsolved questions of doll collectors. They were sent to England and the United States to illustrate the current styles. Their original dresses were of net whereas today, fashion designs are most often made up in tissue paper.

Miss Anna V. Doyle, a kindergarten teacher of Jamaica Plains, Massachusetts, bought the entire collection of the late Mrs. Hendricks of Worcester, Massachusetts, which included a varied and interesting group of milliners' models. To illustrate the difference of hairdos and sizes, Miss Doyle had a picture taken showing both back and front views.

The milliners' model comes in a variety of sizes from six inches to thirty-six inches—the largest we have seen. Mrs. William Walker of Louisville, Kentucky, has one twenty-six inches tall with the earliest type of hair dressing found among them. In the writer's collection are three tall ones, eighteen inches, twenty-one inches and twenty-six inches. The eighteen and twenty-one-inch dolls came from the Hendricks collection. The woman of the pair has her hair arranged in a knot at the crown of the head with curls on her neck on each side of the knot—an arrangement that makes her a decidedly rare and unusual type.

Through the courtesy of Mrs. Grace Perlberg of New York we have a photograph taken at Miss Helen Walter's Just Folks Doll House at Stanton, Virginia, showing the number and variety of papier-mâché heads available in that shop.

The Germans were pre-eminent in the making of papier-mâché though, of course, the majority of papier-mâché heads we see in America were made by Ludwig Greiner of Philadelphia, patented in 1858 and again in 1872.

That Greiner made dolls before the date of his first patent in 1858 is quite clear from three unusual papier-mâché heads which have all the earmarks of a Greiner doll. They have painted eyes and on the left shoulder have printed in black letters three-quarters of an inch high: "PATENT APPLIED FOR."

Mrs. Edmund Poetter's doll shown here is all original and is quaintly dressed in black. The work on the head is a little more crude, perhaps, than that of the marked Greiner heads, but no more than might be expected in a first attempt at a product. One can easily detect the master hand in the doll. This makes it easy to see that the manufacture of his dolls was extended beyond the end of his own work in 1872. In *The Dolls of Yesterday* is the picture of a doll found in Burlington, Vermont, in original clothes of the 1870-1880 period which bears evidence of having had a label of the same size and shape as the Greiner label on its left shoulder while on the right shoulder it retains a white paper label reading "Unbreakable without linen." Of course one of the selling points of the original Greiner was that it was unbreakable because reënforced by linen. To be "unbreakable without linen" would seem to represent an improvement over the old process.

But earlier than any Greiner, were the German-made papier-mâché "pre-Greiner" dolls in various sizes, having blown glass eyes. These dolls were probably made from 1835 to 1845. Most of them have their hair arranged behind their ears, leaving the ears exposed. A group of five dolls in this model in various sizes from the collections of Mrs. Edmund Poetter of Reading, Vermont, and Mrs. Ralph E. Wakeman of Claremont, New Hampshire, gives one a pretty clear idea of the sizes. A still smaller size than any of these is in the collection of the Tryphosa Bassett House in Dennisport, Massachusetts.

Mrs. Edmund Poetter has in her collection of rare dolls several variations of the German glass-eyed doll. For instance she has two which have real hair wigs. Ordinarily the papier-mâché head is molded and it is only very occasionally that one runs across such a head with a hair wig. Mrs. Poetter also has a papier-mâché doll with so-called "flirting eyes," that is, eyes that move from side to side instead of up and down. This doll is at least one hundred years old and is all original, including its clothing.

A papier-mâché doll with a head which also appears in china, both blonde and brunette, is "Minnie" in the collection of Mrs. Lydia Bowerman of Port Clinton. These heads were undoubtedly made in Germany, about 1860 and were probably imported and assembled in this country.

Charming and quite unusual is a papier-mâché head with long curls, among the dolls of Mrs. Clarence Medlock of Gloversville, New York, whose collection is extremely well selected.

Not all papier-mâché doll heads were made in Germany or in America. One doll, something on the style of a milliners' model, has a history that places it in Italy. The facial type is distinctly Italian and so are the clothes. The body, legs and arms are of homespun linen and pinned to the doll is a piece of paper which is inscribed:

ITALIAN DOLL

Doll given to Lydia Stone Channing
In Rome, Christmas 1849

A great mystery to doll collectors has been the stamp, "Holtz-Masse" on many different types of dolls. No one has been able to secure any information on a doll maker of that name. The number and variety of types on which this name has appeared has led to the belief that Holtz-Masse was not a doll maker but a jobber who bought and sold the dolls of various makers. Tending to prove this is a doll in the collection of Mrs. Courtney Edmond of Clifton Forge, Virginia, which bears on its body the stamp "Holtz-Masse" and also the name and address of the maker with the patent date, 1874. The latter information is also stamped on the body just under the right arm.

Group of milliners' models
Collection of Miss Anna V. Doyle, Jamaica Plains, Massachusetts

Group of milliners' models, rear view
Collection of Miss Anna V. Doyle, Jamaica Plains, Massachusetts

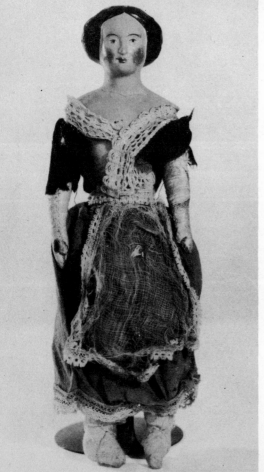

Milliners' models of unusual size, *left to right*, 18 inches, 26 inches and 21 inches tall
St. George Collection

Earliest type of milliners' model, twenty-six inches tall
Collection of Mrs. William Walker, Louisville, Kentucky

Pre-Greiner dolls with blown glass eyes
Collections of Mrs. Edmund H. Poetter,
    Reading, Vermont, and Mrs. Ralph
    E. Wakeman, Claremont, New
    Hampshire

Italian papier-mâché head on doll similar
    to milliners' model
St. George Collection

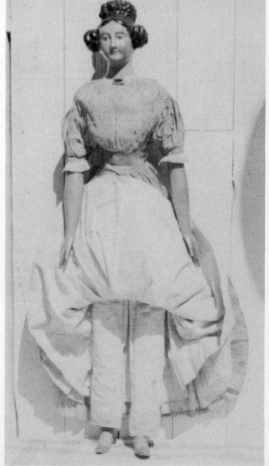

1

2

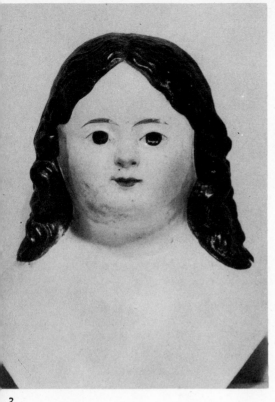

3

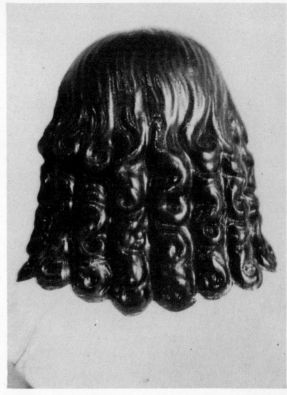

4

1. Papier-mâché dolls from Miss Helen
   Walter's Just Folks Doll House
Courtesy of Mrs. Grace A. Perlberg,
   New York, New York

2. Group of papier-mâché dolls
Collection of Mrs. Byron Peckham,
   Yorkshire, New York

3. Rare papier-mâché head with hairdo
   of long curls
Collection of Mrs. Clarence Medlock,
   Gloversville, New York

4. Rare papier-mâché head, back view
Collection of Mrs. Clarence Medlock,
   Gloversville, New York

5. All original, old "flirting eye" doll of
   papier-mâché. Eyes move from side
   to side
Collection of Mrs. Edmund H. Poetter,
   Reading, Vermont

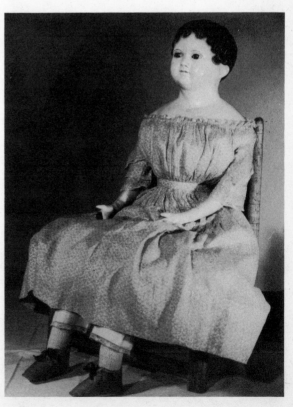

5

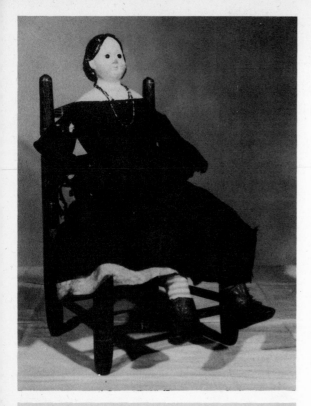

Left,
Probably the earliest Greiner papier-
 mâché doll, before 1858 patent.
 Only three known dolls of this type
Collection of Mrs. Edmund H. Poetter,
 Reading, Vermont

Facing page,
"Minnie," large papier-mâché doll
Collection of Mrs. Lydia Bowerman,
 Milan, Ohio

Left,
Back view of old Greiner doll
Collection of Mrs. Edmund H. Poetter,
 Reading, Vermont

Facing page,
Pair of unusual old papier-mâché dolls
 with wigs
Collection of Mrs. Edmund H. Poetter,
 Reading, Vermont

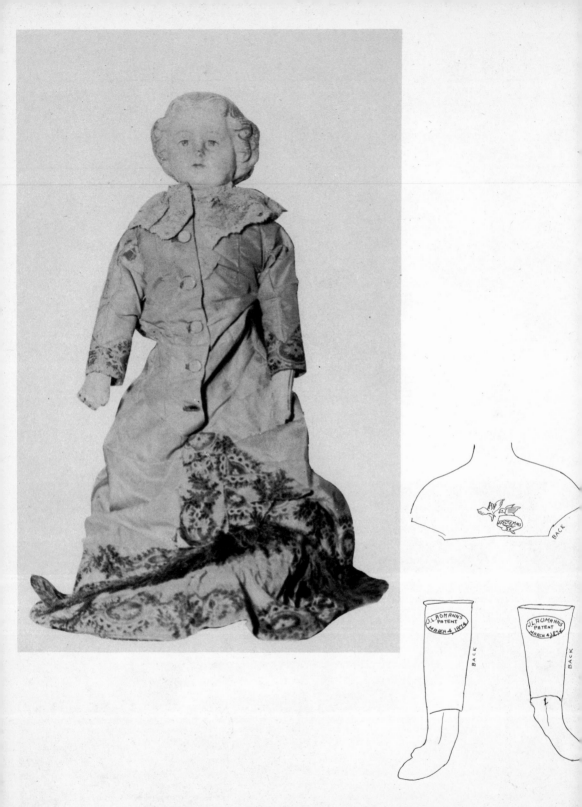

Holtz-Masse composition doll, also bearing the maker's name
Collection of Mrs. Courtney Edmond, Clifton Forge, Virginia

15

Montanari Dolls

THE fulfillment of a childhood dream and a promise made to herself more than forty years before came to Miss Laura Coombs Hills of Newburyport, Massachusetts, as she stood in a London toy shop, a few hours before sailing for home, saw and then purchased a lovely dark-haired Montanari wax doll, the only one in the toy shop, and by the date, very likely the only one of its kind still for sale in any London shop. At the suggestion of her English friend she called the doll "Patricia" for the royal princess, the Princess Patricia of Connaught, who was then much in the news.

Miss Hills sailed happily for her home in America with her new possession, dreaming of the lovely clothes she would make for the doll. Even seasickness did not mar her dreams. That was forty years ago and Miss Hills, now ninety, still has the doll, which she is planning to give to the Historical Society Museum of Newburyport.

Miss Hills decided to dress her doll in wonderful handmade underwear trimmed with real lace, a white satin corset, and a hoop made from a real hoop skirt she had in the attic. Then came the lovely three-flounced pink dress, each flounce being scalloped and bound with a darker pink ribbon called "Pompadour." Then came an exquisite bonnet and a black Chantilly lace mantle.

Miss Hills decided that Patricia, when fully dressed, must have a "coming-out party" so she invited fourteen little boys and girls, asking the girls to bring their dolls and the boys to bring their Teddy Bears. Patricia received standing on a table against a background of green silk, looped with tiny pink rosebuds. Around her feet were little vases of flowers. When the children came they all brought presents for Patricia. She poured tea at a small table and the children sat on the floor to drink it. As their stomachs were full size, they also were given ice cream and cake. Cookies half an inch wide and cups of tea were not enough to satisfy them. One small boy, age five, who had very tight pants, said they were new and white and he would *not* sit on the floor, and another small boy was heard to boast that his sister's doll had a new dress for the party.

Each little girl was given a real water-color miniature of Patricia, painted by Miss Hills, to hang around her own doll's neck. One of these miniatures, painted thirty-five years ago, which was sent to this writer by Miss Hills recently, will be one of her most treasured possessions.

A native of Newburyport, Miss Hills was born in 1859 and is a miniature artist of world fame. She has won, among other honors, the medal of Art Interchange 1895; Paris Exposition 1900, Second Prize; Corcoran Art Gallery, Washington, D. C. 1901; Silver Medal Buffalo Exposition, 1901; Gold Medal St. Louis Exposition 1904; and many other prizes. Her work is in many art museums, including the Boston Museum of Fine Arts.

Recently Patricia and her accessories were displayed in the specially decorated window of a Newburyport department store.

Judging by her age, Patricia was undoubtedly made by Mme. Montanari's son, and is probably one of the last dolls that he made. The unique methods of the Montanaris, mother and son, were first recognized when their dolls were shown at the Crystal Palace Exposition in 1851 and again in the Paris Exposition in 1854. Mme. Augusta Montanari is credited with having introduced the first child dolls. Previously all dolls were women.

They made a thick wax doll with hairs set individually in its head with a hot needle, very successfully simulating the human scalp. Possibly the method of putting hair on wax dolls was not original with the Mon-

Facing page,
Patricia—a Montanari wax doll
Courtesy of Laura Coombs Hills, Newburyport, Massachusetts

Patricia, her wardrobe and accessories on display in a Newburyport store window
Courtesy of Laura Coombs Hills, Newburyport, Massachusetts

tanaris because there is a pair of small wax dolls in the Guyotte Museum at Peterborough, New Hampshire, in which the hair is inserted in the wax in groups of three or four hairs together at intervals of about half an inch apart and arranged in rows about three quarters of an inch apart. Mrs. Edmund Poetter of Reading, Vermont, has a similar doll. Of course this may have been an early experiment of the Montanaris or it may be the work of an earlier doll artist. The hair has all been cut off by moths but enough remains to show the method and placement.

Very little is known about the Montanaris themselves and that little is mostly from the advertisements in the business section of the London Post Office Directory in the Library of Congress. The father, Napoleon Montanari, was an artist and a modeller of wax figurines.

How carefully one must check on the stories that accompany old dolls is well illustrated by a recent purchase of the author's. The doll in question is a genuine Mme. Augusta Montanari which was bought from Mrs. R. P. Fitts of Keene, New Hampshire, when she sold her collection

Doll by Mme. Augusta Montanari, mistakenly called the Hawthorne doll
St. George Collection

a few years ago. Mrs. Fitts had bought the doll four years earlier through a mail auction of a dealer in Salem, Massachusetts. The dealer claimed she was acting for the original owner, an old lady who was breaking up her home on account of ill health. Mrs. Fitts received the doll accompanied by the following letter, purportedly from the original owner—as indeed it may have been. No address was given and the letter was dated October 1, 1940.

"Dear Mrs. Fitts:

"I have received your check through our mutual friend. I am now turning over to you the ownership of the wax doll. It first was my sister's doll.

"It was purchased abroad by my uncle, Nathaniel Hawthorne, in 1860 in May. It was then dressed in white lawn and had boots that were different. My dear sister was ill at the time and died a year later of consumption. The doll was put away until my tenth birthday, 1869. She was given a new wardrobe at that time, my mother's dressmaker, Alice Smith, being hired to do it.

"I hope you will receive as much happiness from owning her as I have. If it was not for poor health, I would not part with her.

"I have always called her Amelia. I used to pretend she was my sister, reincarnated. I still have this feeling about her and have been very particular who should have her.

"I hope I shall live long enough to meet you. Our friend says such nice things about you. Good day, until we meet.

Alice Hawthorne"

Mrs. Fitts accepted the letter at its face value and assumed that the writer was a niece of Nathaniel Hawthorne, the author. Mrs. Fitts intended to visit the elderly woman but later was told she had passed away.

The story in the letter was plausible enough. There was only one thing wrong with it: namely, that Nathaniel Hawthorne never had any nieces or nephews. The library of the Salem Institute confirms this fact. It also confirms the letter's statement that Nathaniel Hawthorne had been in England in 1860. They were unable to find the name of Alice Hawthorne in their directories. They suggested that we contact Mr.

Manning Hawthorne of Woodstock, Connecticut, Nathaniel Hawthorne's great-grandson. We did, and the following is Mr. Hawthorne's letter, in part:

"I know of no Alice Hawthorne who lived during the time. You ask of Nathaniel Hawthorne's nieces and nephews. As the people at the Institute stated, he had only two sisters, Elizabeth and Louisa, and neither of them ever married. Nor is there any Alice Hawthorne in any of the genealogical tables of the Hawthorne families to my knowledge. So she could not have been a cousin. In all his writings, he never mentioned such a person and if he were bringing a doll to her or her sister, it seems to me that he would have mentioned it.

"My relationship to Nathaniel Hawthorne is great-grandson. My grandfather was Nathaniel Hawthorne's son Julian; my father was his son, John. The only descendants of Nathaniel Hawthorne who are living are the children, grandchildren and great grandchildren of Julian Hawthorne. His elder daughter never married and the young daughter, Rose, married George Parsons Lathrop and had one son who died at the age of five. There are no more descendants of Nathaniel Hawthorne alive today. If Miss Alice Hawthorne had an uncle Nathaniel who brought her a doll in 1860, he was not the author, and no direct kin of the author."

This seemed to put a definite end to any connection between the doll and the author of *The Scarlet Letter* and *The House of Seven Gables*. Efforts were made to locate the woman who had sold the doll, but she had left Salem and no one seemed to know where she had gone. Twenty letters sent out to postmasters, police departments, antique dealers were without avail.

So the doll is valuable strictly for its own merits, without a history. It is clearly from the master hand of Mme. Augusta Montanari. We do not know when she ceased to make dolls, as certain informative volumes of the London Post Office Directory are not in the files of the Library of Congress, but the dolls made by her son are as beautiful and valuable as hers because he continued to use the methods of his mother.

The beautifully modelled features of the "Hawthorne" doll are a rich cream color with age and she has those clear violet-blue eyes found only in the older dolls. Her light chestnut brown hairs are set in individually with a hot needle. She has a cloth body with leather arms.

Her low-cut dress looks as if it had really been made by "my mother's dressmaker, Alice Smith." It is of reseda green silk and in plaid of the same shade. She carries a silk covered basket in which is an ivory fan and an ivory mirror.

A fine example of the work of Mme. Montanari's son is found in the beautiful bride doll from the collection of Mrs. Jean Halter, Philadelphia. The doll is in all particulars like the Mme. Montanari dolls except that the eyes are light blue. It can be dated by the label of F. Aldis whom the available London Post Office Directories in the Library of Congress show was in business until 1890. The doll probably was made in the 1870-1880 decade, judging by its clothing. The elaborate underwear and corset are machine made, thus placing it after 1869, as sewing machines were not commonly used before that time. The dress is of very elegant material, probably from the owner's wedding dress or a court presentation gown. It is made in bustle style with much beautiful lace. The satin in the dress is ivory in tone, and the train is of beautiful cut velvet which, like the satin, has grown ivory in tone. This cut velvet further dates the doll, for the writer has a black dolman of similar material that was worn by her mother in the early 1880's.

On the body of the doll is stamped the label of the seller, Mr. Aldis, which is here reproduced with the picture of the doll.

Stamp of London dealer on body of Mrs. Halter's Montanari doll
Courtesy of Mrs. Jean Halter, Philadelphia, Penna.

Facing page,
Bride doll of 1870-1880 by Montanari, fils
Collection of Mrs. Jean Halter, Philadelphia, Penna.

16

Pedlar Dolls

THE carved wood, jointed pedlar dolls of eighteenth-century England were the expression in dolls of a social institution, portraying as they did the pedlar women or "Notion Nannies" who in that period wandered about the English countryside selling small articles and notions.

A lovely English pedlar doll which dates to about 1780 is especially treasured by the author because it came from three college classmates at the Pennsylvania College for Women in Pittsburgh, Mrs. John M. Phillips, Mrs. John M. Irwin and Miss Anna Rogers Hunt..When we graduated, the classes were small and the warm friendships of our college days have persisted through the years; we have all seemed more like sisters than friends. This gift doll is typical of the jointed pedlar doll. She wears a dress of green and white striped flannel, figured with red flowers and draped over a heavy quilted petticoat of black silk. On her head is a black scoop bonnet over the white mob cap that these pedlar women wore.

It was a full century or so before the English kind of pedlar made an appearance in this country. Some of us will remember the pack pedlars of the 1870's, 1880's and 1890's but these, however, were never commemorated by dolls.

The eighteenth century English pedlar doll did not invariably have a wooden head, though the body and limbs almost always were wood. Mr. and Mrs. Grant Holt have a rare and interesting one with a wax head, the wax being black and the features those of a crone—almost of a witch. The doll was bought from Mrs. Elsie Clark Krug.

Through the courtesy of B. H. Leffingwell of Rochester, New York, we are able to show the picture of the all-metal clock pedlar, which is evidently German. It is unusual and probably the only one of its kind in existence.

In nineteenth-century England the pedlar women continued to be seen in the country lanes and pedlar dolls have continued to be made. Since the year 1860, the women are no longer seen but there is something about the pedlar doll with her miniature wares, that appeals so strongly to the doll makers' and doll collectors' imaginations that they have been made with all sorts of heads—bisque, china, composition, and what have you. There is even a doll type made of fabric by the Bernard Ravcas. This unique pedlar doll was made in 1938 for their first American department store exhibit at Lord & Taylor's in New York. The companion piece to this pedlar woman is the organ grinder we mentioned in Chapter 1 whose organ plays the French National Anthem.

Two of the most beautiful of modern pedlar dolls are in the collection of Mrs. Rudolph C. Siebert of Rochester, New York. They are by Dorothy W. Heizer whose work is known to collectors everywhere for its beauty and meticulous attention to detail.

An unusual development of the pedlar doll idea is in the possession of Mrs. Mary Walton of Philadelphia. About seventy years ago an aunt in Germany was informed of the coming visit from her young niece whom she had never seen. Determined to prepare for the beloved little visitor a wonderful gift, she set to work with needle, thread and scissors on many small articles for sale. She called in the village carpenter and had him construct in miniature an open market stand such as that used by grownups in the town on market day. The whole thing folded up and could be loaded on a small wagon at night. There are four shelves and a counter shelf and numerous hooks on which to hang merchandise. There is need for plenty of space on shelves and counter, for there are 179 miniature articles being offered for sale. A small shingle roof, sloping back, is over all. Behind the counter stands the bisque doll merchant with blue blown glass eyes and white hair piled high on her head. This is not the original doll—she is a replacement.

The 179 articles include: thirteen hats in straw, silk, velvet, lace and

Rare German clock pedlar of tin
Courtesy of B. H. Leffingwell, Rochester, New York

wool; three pairs of shoes, three dozen cakes of soap, nine strings of beads on cards, one half dozen hair bows on cards, one dozen umbrellas, one half dozen white kid gloves, eight rolls of silk ribbon, four pocket books or bags, five dresses, one basket work holder with numerous pieces of veiling, one bisque doll baby in a bunting, and other items too numerous to mention.

The little red boxes to hold the merchandise are marked in old German script. It is amazing how carefully the merchandise—mostly handmade—has been preserved in such clean condition. The bazaar is really a museum piece.

German Bazaar, 1870
Courtesy Mrs. Mary Walton,
Philadelphia, Penna.

Pedlar woman made in 1938
Courtesy Bernard M. Ravca,
New York, New York

Above left,
Modern pedlar doll made by
    Heizer
Collection of
    Mrs. Rudolph C. Siebert,
    Rochester, New York

Above right,
Modern pedlar doll by Heizer
Collection of
    Mrs. Rudolph C. Siebert,
    Rochester, New York

To the left,
Old pedlar doll of about 1780
St. George Collection

Parian Dolls

PARIAN dolls with blown glass eyes are comparatively rare and Parian dolls with swivel necks are even more rare. Seldom indeed do we find the two features combined as in the lovely Parian, "Harriet," from the collection of Mrs. Edna Fletcher of Newburgh, New York. It is outstanding even in so large and fine a collection of rare ceramic dolls as Mrs. Fletcher has.

Another unusual Parian in the same collection has a curl molded on top of the head and four curls molded behind each ear. The doll also has a molded guimpe.

Mrs. Fletcher's collection is not only full of unusual dolls but it is also notable for being one of the best dressed collections in America. All the dolls are costumed in old materials by Mrs. Ralph Wakeman whose skill and taste are undeniable.

The rear view of a doll whose hairdress seems to indicate a date of about 1870 is from the collection of Mrs. Martin Anderson of Worcester, Massachusetts. Note the wreath in the hair, which is quite unusual.

Also from Worcester comes a collection of Parian heads of types quite often seen. They belong to Mrs. Charles Doherty. Mrs. Doherty's already good doll collection was enriched by the lovely dolls she inherited from her friend and neighbor, Mrs. Grace Garland of Worcester. Mrs. Garland was long a collector and dealer in dolls.

The doll head on the extreme left is supposed to be a portrait of

Empress Eugénie of France. It has a lustre band on its head. There is more than one size in this type and there is also another type of head, differing slightly. Mrs. Poetter has both a large and small head of the first kind and also one of the second.

A sixteen-inch Parian from the collection of Miss Anna Doyle of Jamaica Plains, Massachusetts, completes this group of Parian dolls—all of which are owned in the east. They are truly lovely but the eastern collectors have no monopoly on either beauty or rarity. Witness for instance the lovely and unusual Parian owned by Mrs. Edwin Cook of Tacoma, Washington. The waterfall hairdo dates her about 1859. This is a type of Parian which has never before come to our attention.

It does seem curious that these lovely ceramic heads which are so highly prized and so highly priced today should have been so lightly regarded by their makers. For no mention of them appears in books on the work of the Dresden potteries. There seems little doubt that they were put out as mere advertising novelties and were not considered as serious work.

In our opinion, the all-time high in Parian or blonde bisque heads, either antique or modern, was reached by Mrs. Emma C. Clear in her originals of George and Martha Washington. Mrs. Clear, just before her retirement from business, made a reproduction of the lovely blonde bisque, "Toinette," or Marie Antoinette. Only several of these were made. The first few had but one carved pink rose in their hairdos but each of those made afterwards has three pink roses in her hair. The author is one of the few fortunate owners of this model.

All the lovely replicas of china and blonde bisque dolls which were made by Mrs. Clear and stamped "Clear" have now become collectors' items since they are no longer made. Mrs. Smith, the new owner of the Humpty Dumpty Doll Hospital is making all reproduction dolls, including those formerly made by Mrs. Clear, as "Smith" dolls.

1

2

1. Various types of Parian heads
Collection of Mrs. Charles Doherty,
    Worcester, Massachusetts

2. "Harriet"—rare Parian doll with swivel neck
    and blown glass eyes
Collection of Mrs. Edna Fletcher,
    Newburgh, New York

3. Parian doll with unusual hairdress and
    molded yoke
Collection of Mrs. Edna Fletcher,
    Newburgh, New York

3

1

2

3

1. Rear view of a Parian doll with unusual hairdress
Collection of Mrs. Martin Anderson, Worcester, Massachusetts

2. Parian doll in old taffeta
Collection of Miss Anna V. Doyle, Jamaica Plains, Massachusetts

3. George and Martha Washington, Emma C. Clear's own copies of
   the Parian masterpieces
Courtesy of Mrs. Emma C. Clear, Redondo Beach, California

Right,
Rare Parian doll with waterfall hairdress

Below,
Rare Parian doll with water-
fall hairdress, side view
Collection of
Mrs. Edwin Cook,
Tacoma, Washington

Some German Bisques and Porcelains

IT would be difficult to enumerate all the makers of bisque doll heads that are and have been cast in Germany. No finer has probably ever been made than the Royal Kaestner which was made about fifty years ago. Then, in a cheaper doll, there were heads made by Armand Marseilles of the same period.

Three such dolls with kid bodies were a gift to our collection from our friend, Miss Caroline Wright, a psychiatrist of the State Hospital in Waterbury, Vermont; and our neighbor, Mrs. Walter Wood, gave us an Armand Marseilles of a later period with a composition body. All four of these dolls were the same size, twenty-six inches tall. The ubiquitous clothes moth had been there before us and every one of the four was minus its wig so we sent them, with a quantity of human hair, to Humpty Dumpty Doll Hospital for new hairdos. Your friends are always glad to give you old switches and puffs and your hairdresser will save you hair of any desired shade. So the wig problem may be easily solved. It is a wise move for a doll collector always to keep on hand a supply of human hair.

For the Royal Kaestner, which has brown eyes, we used a wig made of the snow white hair cut from this author's own head. It is a very lovely combination, particularly as the doll was dressed in an old light blue moire taffeta, striped with pale blue satin. There are touches of pale pink at the neck and sleeves and a collar was fashioned of some bits of real pointe de Venise lace. She is very lovely.

Miss Wright had requested that one of her dolls should be dressed in Spanish costume and we had visions of doing her up in flounced black taffeta and a black lace mantilla. At just this time, our friends Dr. Philip Cummings and his wife, Cornelia, of Woodstock, Vermont, brought their house guest to call on us. She was Señorita Ana Maria de Celabarros of Leon, Spain. When Philip Cummings was studying at the University of Madrid, he was also tutor to the royal children of Alphonso XIII, then king of Spain. While Philip was a member of the Spanish household, he formed a warm friendship with the court physician who was the grandfather of Señorita de Celabarros. So it was natural that when she came to America she spent her first weeks as a guest in the Cummings household at Woodstock. She now holds a position as translator with the Spanish Embassy in Washington, D. C.

Ana Maria was enthusiastic over our old dolls and volunteered to dress the proposed Spanish doll in the native costume of her own province of Andalusia, explaining that there were fifty so-called "native Spanish costumes," one for each province. The material of the Andalusian traditional dress for adults is used in various colors with coin spots about the size of a dime. These coin spots, reduced proportionately to doll size, permitted the use of white dotted swiss which was bound with red. A fringed red scarf was put around her neck and red carnations were placed in her hair. The dark hair was dressed Spanish style with a high comb in the center. Señorita Ana Maria took her own gold hoop earrings and put them on the doll. In the doll's hands were put a pair of castanets carved from wood by a week-end visitor of the Cummings, a mechanical engineer from Long Island.

The mantilla was not used because, as Ana Maria explained, it is seldom worn except when going to church and a woman with castanets in her hands certainly would not be going to church!

These two lovely dolls were sent to the National Doll Show at the Charles W. Bowers Memorial Museum at Santa Ana, California, in 1949.

Until Jumeau of Paris began the manufacture of his lovely French bisque doll heads, all ceramic heads were made in Germany. Porcelain and china heads continued to be made there exclusively. Apparently few porcelain heads were made and they are rare in American collections today. Most of these heads were used on French fashion dolls like "Sethany Ann," described among the fashion dolls in *The Dolls of Yes-*

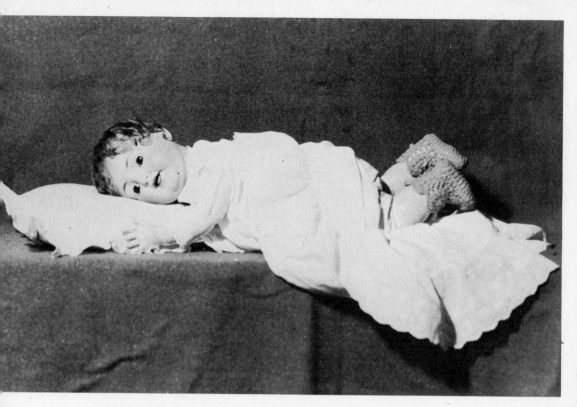

Armand Marseilles baby doll wearing clothes of a human infant
Collection of Mrs. Ralph E. Wakeman, Claremont, New Hampshire

terday. Her garments bear the labels of Mlle. Calixto Huret, who made
and dressed dolls in Paris in the 1850-1860 decade. Another of these is
"Georgiana White," owned by Mrs. Imogene Anderson of New York,
whose wardrobe proclaims her as of the late 1860's. She is shown in
Chapter 7.

"Annie Lee Myers," the twenty-inch porcelain doll from the author's
own collection, is pictured here for her interesting structure. The porcelain head and exquisitely modeled forearms and lower legs came from
Germany. The doll was assembled, however, in Paris, and she bears a
blue patent stamp, "Mme. Rojomer, Paris," showing that the hair-filled,
kid body is French. The name of the patentee is just barely legible. The
porcelain legs and arms are jointed into kid-covered wood which does not
extend all the way to hips or shoulders. The doll's head has a swivel neck
which differs from the French swivel neck invented by M. Jumeau's son.

The doll's head is not open at the crown. Her painted dark blue eyes
are so deep set that they look like glass. Her coloring is lovely and the
dark, human-hair, child's wig hangs long. It was pinned back for the
picture better to display her shoulders.

175

Mrs. Annie Lee Myers, an antique dealer of Port Arthur, Texas, found the doll in a New Orleans attic along with a twenty-inch kid-bodied Jumeau of the 1869 variety. Both dolls seem to have been bought in Paris about 1870 without clothing and then dressed in New Orleans. Their time-yellowed underwear was made by the same loving hands. The Jumeau doll was clothed as a woman in an overskirt dress of brown wool. The child's dress of the porcelain doll is of lace. She had evidently been left without shoes and stockings to show her lovely feet.

Armand Marseilles has also made some lovely baby dolls. One of these, the size of a human baby and wearing real baby clothes, is in the collection of Mrs. Ralph E. Wakeman. Mrs. Wakeman made the wig herself.

Mrs. Emma C. Clear has a friend whose babies had unusually beautiful curls. When the first baby's head was ready for the barber, the mother requested Mrs. Clear to make a doll wig for her of the curls. The hair was too short to weave but after much effort, Mrs. Clear produced a wig which she was not wholly satisfied with. Since selling Humpty Dumpty Doll Hospital, Mrs. Clear has had time for experimentation and has evolved a method of embedding the short hairs in plastic. When the current baby of the family was ready for the barber, the curls were first tied in tiny bunches close to the head before they were cut, thus the curls can be inserted in the plastic, in much the same way as they grow on the child's head. Having leisure now, Mrs. Clear is doing a good deal of experimenting in wax and other mediums.

A doll that is not only much sought after by collectors but which was never very plentiful is the so-called "Blue Scarf Doll." It was once reproduced but the reproduction was not very successful. The doll shown here belongs to Mrs. Alice V. Fredey of Dorchester, Massachusetts. The costume, unfortunately, is an anachronism. It should be of the Empire period since the doll is copied from the famous painting of Queen Louise of Prussia, descending the stairs at Schuenbrun Palace to intercede for her country with the conqueror, Napoleon.

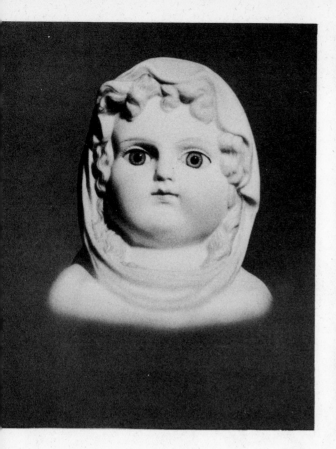

Upper left,
German bisque doll known as the
 "Blue Scarf Doll"
Collection of Mrs. Alice V. Fredey,
 Dorchester, Massachusetts

Upper right,
Annie Lee Myers—porcelain doll
St. George Collection

Right,
Royal Kaestner doll
St. George Collection

Armand Marseilles doll, in authentic Andalusian costume
Costume by Señorita Ana Maria de Celabarros of Leon, Spain
St. George Collection

Doll Dressmaking

WHEN the author of this book and her sister, Frank, two years younger, were small girls, it was a joy to them to nestle down in their mother's bed before going to their own bed at night and listen to the stories suggested to her by the old print in the pieced quilt on her bed. Whose dress had that print been? When was it bought? Where? Who made it? How was it made and where was it first worn?

One of the most fascinating of all to us was the tale of a certain pink print frock that she had worn when a young lady in the early 1870's, on the occasion of first meeting father.

The style in which the dress was made was known as the "pull-back skirt" because most of the fullness in the skirt was in the back breadth and was held in place by a buttoned strap across the back.

We had never seen a "pull-back dress" but when, about two years ago, we received from an up-state New York doll dealer a pair of fourteen-inch "Dolly Madison" type Parian twins, we were sure that their dresses were "pull-backs." Sketching the dress, we sent it to Mrs. Carrie A. Hall, at the Handicraft Shop, North Platte, Nebraska, for confirmation. Mrs. Hall's reply came back quickly, "Yes, that is it."

Through the greater part of her life, Carrie A. Hall was the leading dressmaker for the women of the southwest during the 'eighties, 'nineties and early nineteen hundreds, and there is little worth knowing about the styles of those periods which she cannot tell you. Today, in her eighty-fourth year, Mrs. Hall is applying her skill with these same fashions to the costuming of the wee ladies of the doll world.

One of Mrs. Hall's more recent creations is a series of portrait dolls representing "The First Hundred Years of Women's Progress," which includes such figures as Amelia Bloomer, Sarah Josepha Hale, editor of Godey's, Lucy Stone, Dr. Anna Howard Shaw, Susan B. Anthony, and others. Each of Mrs. Hall's creations has some individual touch. On the author's Amelia Bloomer doll, for instance, the blouse is made from the silk of a parachute used by Mrs. Hall's niece's husband in the South Seas. On her Sarah Josepha Hale doll is a Paisley shawl (which was one of Sarah Josepha's favorite articles of wearing apparel) which was made at the author's request from a square of real handwoven Persian shawl given to us by Mrs. Emma C. Clear. Mrs. Hall crocheted on it a multicolored fringe from old silk of the Civil War period. Such personal touches add to the charm of Mrs. Hall's dolls.

The writer has always been an active worker for women's suffrage since she first, at the age of sixteen, heard Dr. Anna Howard Shaw speak on the subject, and was a member of the Executive Board of the Equal Franchise Federation of Allegheny County in Pennsylvania. It was then that the women of Pennsylvania attempted to pass a suffrage amendment to the Pennsylvania State Constitution, only to be defeated by the political machine of Philadelphia.

When we learned from Mrs. Hall that she had known the real Susan B. Anthony and had once made a dress for her, we asked her to dress our Susan B. Anthony doll in a replica of that dress.

Susan B. Anthony, the suffrage pioneer, was never a "dressy" person. She had weightier matters on her mind—the fight for the rights of women. When in 1894 she went to Kansas to visit her brother, a noted editor, her unfashionable appearance caused a great deal of consternation among her sisters-in-law. A family conclave was hastily arranged and it was agreed that "Susan really *must* have something decent to wear." To that end, they took her to their friend and dressmaker, Mrs. Carrie A. Hall.

One sister-in-law presented Susan with a foundation garment to wear under the new frock—a tan silk petticoat. Remember those silk petticoats in which the ladies of the gay 'nineties used to swish about? Crisp rustling taffeta with an accordion pleated flounce? The dress presented

Right,
Pink print dresses with "pull-back" skirts on Dolly Madison type Parians. Original dresses of 1873
St. George Collection

Below,
Dolls by Mrs. Carrie A. Hall from her series, "The First Hundred Years of Women's Progress." *Left to right:* Lucy Stone, Amelia Bloomer and Sarah Josepha Hale
St. George Collection

problems. Susan was a Quaker so it had to be of Quaker gray. She wore no jewelry, so the dressmaker finished the neck and sleeves with white collar and cuffs and a blue bow at the throat.

The sisters-in-law wanted the dress trimmed in black soutache braid in fashionable curlicues. Susan resisted; she would have no curlicues. Finally they compromised on black soutache braid arranged in straight lines. So the dress for the doll which Mrs. Hall copied not only commemorates Susan but also Mrs. Hall's own adventures in the realm of fashion.

When one is known to have a fondness for old doll clothes, many gifts are apt to come to one, such as the real Persian shawl from Mrs. Clear, mentioned above. One of the most touching gifts came to us recently from Mrs. Harriet Burnham Harvey of Cortland, New York. It was a doll dress made seventy-two years ago by her mother for Mrs. Harvey's first doll. Unfortunately, the original doll had been broken.

"I am sending the dress to you because I know you will preserve it and care for it. I would not sell it to anyone," wrote Mrs. Harvey, who has long been a well-known doll dressmaker and dealer.

One of the joys of having written a doll book comes from letters one receives from other collectors. In the two years following the publication of *The Dolls of Yesterday*, for instance, we have received and answered over two thousand letters. And such bits of information one gains from them! For instance, have you ever heard of knee warmers for a doll? No? Neither did we until the other day when a letter came from Mrs. Grace Toalson of Osceola, Missouri, and in it was a picture of "Hester," knee warmers and all. Hester has an interesting history, as related by Mrs. Toalson:

"Mr. and Mrs. Will Vannice had no children. At Christmas Mr. Vannice would give his wife a doll. The years went by. Mr. Vannice passed away, worldly goods vanished, too, but Hester clung to this doll. Mr. Vannice's brother took her into his home. After Hester Vannice died her sister-in-law gave the doll to my care. So her name is fittingly 'Hester.' How I love her! She is very fine china and is entirely original without a crack or a chip."

From *Harper's Bazaar* of 1869 is a picture illustrating fashions for dolls, which comes by way of Mrs. Emma Clear through the courtesy of Mrs. E. S. Carmick, owner of old copies of the magazine.

Left,
Doll representing Sarah Josepha Hale, editor of Godey's, wearing Paisley shawl made by Mrs. Carrie A. Hall
St. George Collection

Above right,
Doll by Mrs. Carrie A. Hall representing Susan B. Anthony in replica of the dress made by Mrs. Hall for the real Susan B. Anthony in 1894
St. George Collection

Right,
"Hester" and her knee warmers
Collection of Mrs. Grace Toalson, Osceola, Missouri

Doll fashions from *Harper's Bazaar* of 1869
Courtesy of Mrs. Emma C. Clear, Redondo Beach, California

Demorest also furnished styles and patterns for dolls. Mrs. M. H. Cannon of Waldwick, New Jersey, has one of these old patterns in her collection as well as the twenty-one inch doll that was dressed after this pattern. The pattern is in a five-by-six-inch envelope and the following description is printed on the front:

MME. DEMOREST
Paris   New York
New and Stylish Patterns for Dolls
Each set comprises a complete wardrobe
Set No. 1—Breton costume—demi-train skirt
Allows all seams and hems

On the reverse side of the envelope are printed full directions for making the garments.

What dressmaking can do for a doll is shown by one in the collection of Mrs. Curtis Alger of West Lebanon, New Hampshire. This doll was dressed in authentic materials by Mrs. Alger's mother, Mrs. L. J. Gardner of Quechee, Vermont. With the authentic goods, correct styling and

184

"Princess dress" made in 1873 for the doll of a little girl in Woodstock, Vermont
St. George Collection

accessories, she transformed a cheap advertising doll into an incredibly lifelike "lady of the Gay 'Nineties."

When, more than a quarter of a century ago, the unsuccessful Children's Theatre of New York opened—and closed—with a dramatization of Frances Hodgson Burnett's delightful doll story, *Racketty Packetty House*, the scenery and rights to the play were bought by a young stage manager and taken, with three professional children to play the leads, on tour to such cities as Washington and Pittsburgh, the local sponsors providing children for the balance of the cast. In Pittsburgh, sponsored by the College Club of Pittsburgh, among the ten or more performances, there were two free performances in which Carnegie Hall was twice filled with children from settlements and orphanages and institutions for blind and crippled children. Because of this charitable feature, the merchants and business houses were generous in their support. McCreery's Department Store, for instance, donated the use of one of their large display windows for two weeks, the equivalent of about six thousand dollars in advertising. Charles Vosburgh, the head window-dressing specialist, designed a scene from the play depicting the wedding party in front of the church, the principals and guests being represented by dolls. McCreery's millinery department dressed the bride; and the other women in quaint costumes copied from Godey's Ladies Book, were done by members of the College Club. The dress suits of the bridegroom and other men presented something more of a problem, so we appealed to a fashionable men's tailor to cut us a pattern for a dress suit.

When we went for our pattern, the Irish cutter said, "Here is your pattern, madam," and then added a little sheepishly, "Now this little fellah, this Peter Piper, the bridegroom, I've kind o' got interested in the little fellah and if you'll leave him I'll make his suit myself."

Thus it was that the shabby little Peter Piper went to his wedding to the aristocratic Lady Patricia Vere de Vere clad in a suit of fine black broadcloth made by the most fashionable tailor who catered to the Pittsburgh millionaire trade. Thus it was, too, that long before we began to collect dolls, we learned how universal is the human interest appeal of a doll to men and women whatever their status or occupation.

Of human interest, too, is the pale yellow taffeta "Princess dress," chiffon trimmed, in the author's collection of old doll clothes. It was made in 1873 for a little girl of Woodstock, Vermont, by a French maid in the household of the late ex-Governor Billings of Vermont. No doubt it was made by the emigrant girl so that she might create the fashion of her beloved Paris. Probably the doll for which she made it was a French doll.

The dress is in ten gores and is laced up the back with eyelets and cord. The so-called "Princess dress" was created in 1873 by Worth, the famous dressmaker of Paris, for the beautiful Princess of Wales, afterwards Queen Alexandria of England.

20

The Ludlow, Vermont Doll Carriages

JOEL ELLIS of Springfield, Vermont, is reputed to have made the first baby carriages and doll carriages in America. The Ellis factory was later known as the Vermont Novelty Works Company.* But in the matter of doll buggies and toy wagons, he was very closely followed by the Ludlow Toy and Manufacturing Company of nearby Ludlow, Vermont, which issued its first catalogue and price list in 1874. Not many collectors have known about the Ludlow enterprise and some may have these carriages, attributing them to Joel Ellis. Through Miss Ella G. Howe, of Ludlow, the daughter of the late E. L. Howe who was superintendent of the Ludlow Toy and Manufacturing Company, we received the tiny catalogue of the company for the year 1874. This catalogue features just two doll carriages but we have been able to consult the 1886 edition of the catalogue through the courtesy of Mr. Harold Rugg, Assistant Librarian of the Baker Memorial Library, Dartmouth College, Hanover, New Hampshire, who has the catalogue in his fine personal collection of Vermont historical items. In this catalogue are three different types of carriages which are here pictured.

The business was begun in a small way in 1872 by A. B. Briggs and N. Graves on Main Street in Ludlow. It gave employment to eight or

* From M. D. Gilman's "The Bibliography of Vermont," published in Burlington in 1897, is taken the following title: "Annual catalog of Children's Carriages and Toys, manufactured by the Vermont Novelty Works Co., Springfield, Vermont. Organized 1859, washed out, 1864; washed away 1869; burned, June 25, 1878. And 'we still live'."

ten hands. The concern was purchased in the early part of 1873 by a stock company incorporated under the general laws of Vermont. The organization was fully completed May 23, 1873, by the election of the following directors: S. W. Stimson, E. A. Howe, Cyrus Buswell, William H. Walker, and L. E. Sherman. The latter was elected president and E. A. Howe, Clerk.

The capital stock of the corporation was $10,000 which was afterwards increased to $15,000. The new company began business June 10, 1873, in Main Street but on December 1, 1883, moved to their new buildings located in the eastern part of the village, a dam having been built by them on the Black River. The buildings were of wood, thirty-five feet by thirty and, including machinery, cost a total of $16,000. It employed about forty men and the annual production was about $30,000.

The company sold its real estate and business in 1887 to S. W. Stimson, E. A. Howe and William H. Walker who continued the business under the name of The Ludlow Manufacturing Company. They discontinued the making of toys in the spring of 1889 and devoted themselves to the production of lumber and chair stock. The other toys which the Ludlow Toy and Manufacturing Company made, aside from doll carriages, were toy carts and wheelbarrows.

The importance of doll carriages in their scheme of manufacturing is shown from the first by the fact that a doll carriage is pictured on the front cover of each of the two catalogues.

Top left,
Doll carriage by the Ludlow Toy and Manufacturing Company of Ludlow, Vermont. Catalogue of 1874.

Top right,
Doll carriage by the Ludlow Toy and Manufacturing Company of Ludlow, Vermont. Catalogue of 1874.

Right,
Doll carriage by the Ludlow Toy and Manufacturing Company of Ludlow, Vermont. Catalogue of 1886.

On facing page,
Doll carriages by the Ludlow Toy and Manufacturing Company of Ludlow, Vermont. Catalogue of 1886.

21

Dolls in Visual Education

ARE you the visual or the auditory mental type? If you are in doubt about the correct spelling of a word, do you write it down, for instance, and look at it to see if it "looks right," or do you spell it out mentally or audibly to see if it "sounds right?" More than forty years ago, William James, the eminent psychologist of Harvard, stated that all were of one type or the other.

Modern educational systems lean heavily upon this theory and our public schools have many aids which they use in teaching. There are phonograph records and radio programs which they use for the auditory types, and geography and history are taught through such exhibits as dolls in the dress of foreign countries and engaged in typical national occupations and social customs.

Boston University has a fine course for teachers in the use of auditory and visual aids. Many museums, such as the Boston Children's Museum, have departments which lend out such aids to the public schools, as needed.

The San Diego, California, schools are unusually progressive and have acquired what is probably the finest set of costume dolls for visual education in the country. They were made by artists with the W.P.A. during the depression and are notable for their fidelity to racial types and the artistic detail of the native costumes. Those described here are among the groups belonging to the San Diego schools.

An American historical group needs no description—it is an American family of the Civil War period.

In the pictured early American group are:

1. THOMAS, THE TAR—The merchant ship played an important part in early American history. About 1800 the American merchant marine ranked second in the world. Sailors aboard the vessels of that period did not look much like the seamen of today. They wore bow ties with flowing ends, tight-fitting jackets trimmed with brass buttons, and flat-topped hats of black patent leather. Bearded faces were common and a man usually braided his hair into a queue in the back. Like today's seaman, the early tar wore his clothes with a jaunty air.

2. SALTY, THE SAILOR MAN—An American seaman of the late seventeenth century was a dashing figure. More picturesque than the modern sailor, his costume was suggestive of the pirate. Around his trimly fitting doublet was a belt which held his pistol or knife. A bright colored kerchief banded his hair, over which was worn a high fur cap. A white cotton blouse and short boots exposing the bare knees, completed the sailor's costume.

3. PRUDENCE OF THE COLONIES—One of the important tasks of a colonial household was the making of candles. Every bit of tallow was hoarded for this purpose. A natural material for candles was supplied by the waxy berries of the bayberry bush. The commonest method of making candles was by dipping. The housewife spun wicks from hemp or flax. Then she fastened them on to a candle rod and dipped them into a pot of boiling-hot tallow. After cooling the wicks were dipped again and again until they were of the desired size.

4. SIMON, THE PILGRIM DRUMMER—In the days of the Pilgrim Fathers there were no bells to ring out news or call the people together. Instead, public gatherings were announced by beating on a drum. The drummer dressed in the typical costume of his settlement. Pilgrim men wore tight-fitting doublets with capped sleeves. Capes were shorter and narrower than those worn by the Puritans. Knee breeches, low shoes, and a high-crowned hat completed the costume. Later, due to Puritan influence, laws restricting dress were introduced in Massachusetts.

5. BASIL, THE BLACKSMITH—During the colonial era in America, the blacksmith was a very important man. In those days, horses were the chief means of transportation. A blacksmith often traveled from village

American family of the Civil War Period
Courtesy of San Diego Public Schools

to village carrying his small stock of tools by cart. Besides horseshoes, he also made nails and various farm implements. When a blacksmith set up his anvil in a village, his workshop soon became a popular place. Here the curious townspeople loved to gather and ply the occasional stranger with questions about his travels.

From Portugal and Sardinia are:

1. LUIS OF PORTUGAL—Luis is a kelp gatherer. He lives at Esponsende, on the northwest coast of Portugal. He is wearing his work-day clothes. The big wooden rake he carries is for gathering the kelp, or seaweed, from the surf. Grape raisers use the dried kelp for fertilizing their vineyards. Many of Luis' countrymen work in the wineries, and many others are fishermen. Some work in the cork oak forests, gathering cork bark from the trees.

2. ZERLINA OF SARDINIA—Zerlina is the daughter of a prosperous merchant of Osilo, in northern Sardinia. The blood of many races flows in her veins, for this rocky island in the Mediterranean did not always belong to Italy. Women of her district are noted for their rich costumes

192

EARLY AMERICAN TYPES
Left to right: Thomas, the tar; Salty, the sailor; Prudence of the Colonies; Simon, the pilgrim drummer; Basil, the blacksmith, and an American hunter and trapper

Courtesy of San Diego Public Schools

of silks and laces, and Zerlina has put on this gorgeous scarlet dress to attend a festival. The home-woven peasant clothes are known for their durability and fast colors. Mining and fishing are important industries in Sardinia, but the visitor is impressed by the diversity of scene, dress and occupation.

3. LEONORA OF PORTUGAL—Leonora has embroidered the name of her home town on the front of her skirt. The women of her province are noted for their grace and for the beauty of their native costumes. They are extremely clever needlewomen and their dresses are often elaborately embroidered. The native slippers have no backs, and it is a trick to keep them on. Many of the peasant women go barefoot. Some are employed in the wineries, where they tread the grapes with their feet. Their straight backs and graceful walks come from the habit of carrying heavy market baskets or water jars on their heads.

4. TURIDU OF SARDINIA—Turidu lives in Cabras, a village on the west coast of Sardinia, rich in fisheries. In summer he wears this lambskin jacket over his coarse, white linen trousers and loose-necked shirt. The

193

fur is worn on the inside as a protection from malaria, for the land here
is low and marshy. In the end of his long stocking cap Turidu often carries a bit of bread and cheese or other food. The bread is in flat, brittle
cakes, and when broken crumbles into many pieces.

From Northern Europe come:

1. GLEDA—Gleda wears the costume of the Swedish Lapp. She has
on her fanciest bonnet and dress. Like Maja, she wears the white fur
shoes and leggings which are saved for such festive occasions as market
day, or going to church or to a wedding. She wove the red and white
ankle bands herself. The women like the ones Vidar wears.

2. VIDAR—Vidar is from the Norwegian part of Lapland. He has on
his heavy fur pesk, or kapta, which he wears for long trips over the snow.
The coat is made from the long-haired fur of the reindeer's back. His fur
boots are curled up at the toes to keep his skis on. He wears the typical
silver-trimmed belt of the Lapp man, with tobacco pouch attached and
a deer-horn knife. His four-cornered cap is called "the cap of the four
winds."

NORTHERN EUROPE
Left to right: Gleda in costume of Swedish Lapp, Vidar from Norwegian part of
Lapland, Maja from Finnish Lapland, Icelandic man and Frieda of Iceland
Courtesy of San Diego Public Schools

3. MAJA—Maja is from Finnish Lapland. She is old, but she still loves to attend the market day festivities. Perhaps she will get another shawl for her shoulders, or a bright new kerchief to tie over her embroidered cap.

4. ICELANDIC MAN.

5. FRIEDA OF ICELAND—Frieda is the daughter of a prosperous farmer. Her beautiful native dress is made of black velvet. A garland of leaves is embroidered in gold above the hem of the skirt and down the front of the bodice. This holiday costume belonged to Frieda's grandmother. Her great-grandmother wore the silver crown which holds the white veil in place. Such heirlooms are always inherited by the oldest daughter of the family.

From Switzerland and Germany we see:

1. CZECHA OF SWITZERLAND—Czecha wears her most festive clothes to attend a folk dance in the village. She is proud of her full-skirted native dress with its tight bodice and snowy white sleeves. The high-crowned hat with its jaunty feather is typical of the section from which she comes.

195

SWITZERLAND AND GERMANY

Left to right: Czecha of Switzerland, Damion of Tyrol, Charlotta of Bavaria, Rupert von Henzau of Bavaria

Courtesy of San Diego Public Schools

Czecha lives in Tyrol, that beautiful part of Switzerland between Austria and Italy which is know to tourists as "the land of the mountains." The women of Switzerland are noted for their dainty embroideries, which, with the famous Swiss cheeses, form the country's chief exports.

2. DAMION OF TYROL—Damion lives in Innsbruck, chief city of that beautiful part of Switzerland known as Tyrol. He wears this picturesque native costume on feast days to attract the tourist. The black velvet trousers are richly embroidered around the waist. With them he wears bright suspenders and other gaily-colored accessories. Heavy woolen stockings keep his legs warm, and his shoes are embellished with bright silvery buckles. Like his sister, Damion sometimes adds a cluster of flowers and a jaunty feather to his hat.

3. CHARLOTTA OF BAVARIA—Charlotta's home is Schliersee, a mountain village in southern Bavaria. From her window she can see the herd girls on the green-clad hills. Her instinctive love of color is expressed in this dress of varied hues with its gay beads and ornaments. Many Ba-

ALBANIA AND GREECE

Left to right: Valona of Albania, Lulash of Albania, Zarkos of Athens and Gaia of
Epirus
Courtesy of San Diego Public Schools

varian women have gone into business since the World War, but in the villages their chief occupation is still that of caring for the home.

4. RUPERT VON HENZAU OF BAVARIA—Rupert, who was named in honor of the Bishop of Worms who introduced Christianity into Bavaria, lives in a chalet type of house like those in Switzerland. He earns his living by guiding tourists to various places of scenic and historic interest. Like his neighbors in the mountain villages, he wears the native costume, but in Munich and other industrial centers of Bavaria this picturesque style of dress is being replaced by modern apparel.

In the Mediterranean region we have from Albania and Greece:

1. VALONA OF ALBANIA—Valona has put on her prettiest dress, for she expects a visit from some American tourists. She will serve them with a lump of Turkish delight, or loukoum, and very sweet coffee. She lives in Scutari, on the northwestern coast of Albania, among a clan of costume makers. The material in their sleeveless jackets is often completely covered by elaborate embroidery. The extremely full trousers require ninety square feet of cloth. When Valona is married she will receive a

197

chest, or dunti, from the bridegroom's family, containing clothing, ornaments, coffee and a large loaf of sugar.

2. LULASH OF ALBANIA—Lulash acts as guide to the timid visitors
whose travels take them through wild mountain passes. The style of his
costume indicates his home region, for in Albania each clan is distin-
guished by its mode of dress. Wide sashes, sometimes fifteen feet in
length, are worn by all the men, wrapped many times about their waists.
These serve as pockets for cigarettes and other small articles. Agriculture
is the chief occupation of this small kingdom whose people represent
southeastern Europe's most ancient race.

3. ZARKOS OF ATHENS—Zarkos belongs to the Presidential Guard. His
stiff, pleated skirt of linen or cotton is the fustenella, the national costume of Greece. The short buttoned jacket and the cap with a tassel
complete the costume. Albania once owned Greece. Otto, the first king
of the new Greece, wore this uniform, as did all his royal retinue. Today,
only the presidential guard and a few rugged shepherds wear the fustenella.

4. GAIA OF EPIRUS, GREECE—Gaia embroidered her festival dress by
hand. She wears a tight belt with the wool skirt. Her necklace and buckle
are gold. The beaded turban is like the one Queen Amilia wore. Beneath
the turban Gaia winds her braids with the ends twisted into a Grecian
knot. Gaia lives in Epinnia, a city in the mountains of Epirus, Greece.
Epirus is a district of tall mountains and great rivers in the northern part.
Once Epirus raised cattle, horses and dogs, now the sturdy mountain
people raise wheat, fruit, vegetables, olives and tobacco.

Whether dolls have been made for educational purposes, made
simply for recreation, or created as works of art, it will readily be seen
that they play very definite roles. The pleasure they have brought to an
untold number of persons warrants their being loved and preserved
from century to century.

Index

no —	61 —	15.00	
no —	62	20.00	
no —	63	10.00	
no —	64 —	10.00	
no —	65	8.00	
no —	66	10.00	
no —	67	15.00	
no —	68 —	10.00	
no —	69 —	10.00	
no —	70 —	10.00	
no —	71 —	10.00	
no —	72 —	12.00	
no —	73 —	5.00	
no —	74	15.00	
no —	75	16.00	Horse shoe Doll
no —	76	15.00	
no —	77	20.00	
no —	78	5.00	
no —	79	5.00	Frozen charlotte
no —	80	10.00	Sticks and Feathers
no —	81	10.00	Boy Doll
no —	82	3.00	pasty Doll
no —	83	4.00	
no —	84	20.00	
no —	85	2.00	
no —	86	9.00	
no —	87	70.00	Colored
no —	88	15.00	
no —	89	(89 and 90	Cost 100.00
no —	90	(84 and 90	
no —	91	75.00	
no —	92	30 nussen head	